THE PRAYERS OF THE NEW MISSAL

The Prayers of the New Missal

A Homiletic and Catechetical Companion

Anscar J. Chupungco

LITURGICAL PRESS
Collegeville, Minnesota

www.litpress.org

For Bishop Julius S. Tonel, DD, SLL
Chairman, Episcopal Commission on Liturgy
Catholic Bishops' Conference of the Philippines

Contents

Foreword

It is for me a bittersweet duty to offer this foreword to Fr. Anscar Chupungco's commentary on selected orations found in the new English translation of the *Missale Romanum* 2002/2008: sweet, because it provides me the opportunity to introduce readers to one of the giants of liturgical scholarship in the latter half of the twentieth century and the beginning of the twenty-first; bitter, because this is the last monograph we will have from Fr. Anscar's pen, since he unexpectedly died on January 9, 2013.

I had the great privilege of knowing Fr. Anscar in many of his roles. He was the first official of the Pontificio Istituto Liturgico to welcome me to the Ateneo Sant'Anselmo on the Aventine Hill in Rome for graduate studies when I began there in 1987; he would also kindly sign my diploma when I completed doctoral studies there in 1991. I had already read Fr. Anscar's groundbreaking study of paragraphs 37–40 of the Constitution on the Sacred Liturgy titled *Cultural Adaptation of the Liturgy*, so I was very curious to know what the author would be like. Over the next four years, I saw him operate as a prudent administrator, giving long service as president of the Pontifical Liturgical Institute as well as serving as rector magnificus of the entire Athenaeum of Saint Anselm. I experienced him as a fine teacher, guiding students from many language groups and ethnic backgrounds in the imaginative reconstruction of Christian worship with careful attention to placing the surviving unwritten and written monuments in their cultural contexts. But though he was meticulous in his attention to historical detail, he was never a mere antiquarian, always seeking to place historical conversation in conversation with theology and the social sciences for the sake of the worshiping church. I delighted in his generosity in encouraging students to become colleagues by inviting them to write scholarly articles for his various projects and was deeply honored when he asked me to make some contributions to the five-volume

Handbook for Liturgical Studies produced under his editorship. But perhaps most importantly, I was edified by celebrating the liturgy when he presided and preached. It was so clear that Fr. Anscar's scholarship was not separate from his life as a priest and a monk, but served the people of God who worshiped liturgically, and this integration offered a model for those of us who also sought to serve God's people as scholars and liturgical ministers.

The qualities that made him such a fine scholar, teacher, and liturgist are powerfully on display in the present work.

First of all, Fr. Anscar calls on the finest resources to offer his interpretation of the underlying Latin texts. His endnotes alone introduce the reader to some of the finest scholarship on liturgical Latin (Mohrmann, Ellebracht, Blaise), Roman orations/collects (Leachman and McCarthy), and interpretation theory (De Zan). He then employs this erudition fruitfully by presenting the present English translation, indicating what may be a difficulty in interpretation, examining the underlying Latin to clarify the meaning, offering a more literal translation, and then giving the sense of the problematic phrase. Here we see a master teacher exemplifying a method of interpretation; wise students could then employ this method to interpret other presidential texts from the Missal for deeper insight.

Second, although he does not shy away from controversy, Fr. Anscar does so in a prudential and irenic way. I don't think it comes as a shock to anyone to learn that the present official English translation of the Roman Missal has had a troubled reception. Rather intense polemics have addressed the replacement of *Comme le Prévoit* with *Liturgiam Authenticam* as the official set of guidelines for translation of liturgical texts, simplistically presented as a choice between "dynamic equivalence" and "formal correspondence" as the fundamental theory of translation. Notice Fr. Anscar's evenhanded assessment of this topic: "Both methods are valid means to translate a text. . . . It would therefore be a biased judgment to dismiss the new translation purely as an exercise on literal translation."

Perhaps most importantly, the aim of the work is pastoral: "to assist priests and catechists to develop the message of the orations in the new English Missal." Although he could have dazzled readers with his command of medieval Latinity and the sometimes convoluted syntax of Latin collects, Fr. Anscar wears his learning lightly, only offering the details needed to clarify his meaning. He knew that, while liturgical preaching is usually inspired by the Scriptures proclaimed, it may also derive from the liturgical texts themselves, and the proper texts of a given formulary (including the presidential prayers) often provide a particular focus for the prayer of the assembly. He also knew that an underdeveloped aspect of the implementation of the Rite of Christian Initiation of Adults is the entire area of sacramental mystagogy. His homiletic-catechetical notes provide rich resources for preachers and those called to deepen the liturgical experience of the baptized.

The Prayers of the New Missal: A Homiletic and Catechetical Companion is a suitable swan song for Fr. Anscar's published works. Here his scholarship is once again put at the service of those leading the church's worship. Here his commitment to the Lord in monastic life, like his Benedictine forebears Prosper Guéranger and Adrien Nocent, offers depths of spiritual insight to a wider public. Here, like the wise steward of Matthew's gospel, Fr. Anscar brings out treasures both new and old.

J. Michael Joncas

St. Paul, Minnesota
Good Friday, 2013

Introduction

"It is the task of the homily and of catechesis to set forth the meaning of the liturgical texts." With these words the instruction *Liturgiam Authenticam* (29) assigns to priests and catechists the duty of explaining what might not be immediately obvious in liturgical texts translated according to the method of formal correspondence. This 2001 instruction requires exact translation without omission, addition, paraphrase, or gloss. However, it foresees that in the process literal translation, which seeks to be faithful to words, phrases, and the word order of the source language, will bring about a new generation of vernacular languages in the liturgy.

My chief aim in producing this book is to assist priests and catechists to develop the message of the orations in the new English Missal. I confine my attention to the presidential prayers—namely, the Collect, Prayer over the Offerings, Prayer after Communion, and a couple of other unique prayers offered by the presider. I deal only with texts whose meaning is not immediately obvious. It is not my intention to review and comment on each oration.

My other aim is to provide methodological tools for interpreting some knotty passages in the new English Missal, excepting the Order of Mass itself.[1] The method consists of examination of the original Latin formularies, analysis of their grammatical construction and vocabulary, and a provisional literal translation in aid of easier comprehension.

I conclude the analysis of the orations with homiletic-catechetical notes.[2] They are samples. It will not be an exaggeration to say that every oration in the Roman Missal has a rich message to convey. Beneath the simplicity and brevity of the Latin text lie hidden gems of doctrine and spirituality: we need to discover them. I focus my attention on a few orations whose sense is not immediately clear in both source and receptor languages. All other orations are waiting to be explored.

In fairness to the new English translation, it needs to be said that the number of difficult orations are relatively few, if we consider that the entire Missal is about fifteen hundred pages long. Sometimes, too, some of the Latin orations, especially those that date from the sixth century, require special hermeneutic study because of their culturally bound vocabulary.[3] There are difficult passages in Latin, and consequently also in the translations. Recent compositions are generally easier to translate.

The difficulty of easy comprehension arises also from the use of the method of formal correspondence, one of whose consequences is the emergence of a new generation of English in the liturgy. As a matter of fact, literal translation can present more challenges than dynamic equivalence. The former tries to preserve the words, phrases, and even word order of the source language in view of communicating the message fully and faithfully. It is a noble undertaking, but the translator has the unenviable task of safeguarding the character of the receptor language.

The latter, on the other hand, works to convey the principal message of the Latin orations clearly and without need of much explanation. However, in the process, some words and phrases in the source language are not carried over in translation, since the concern of the translator is the communication of the message more than the preservation of Latin words and phrases.

Both methods are valid means to translate a text. It should be noted that there are instances when formal correspondence is required, because the text states a doctrine of faith. In my examination of the new English Missal I came across several examples of dynamic equivalence. It would therefore be a biased judgment to dismiss the new translation purely as an exercise on literal translation.

The new translation should not be a cause for disenchantment. With the passing of time, priests and people will become familiar with the literary style of the texts. Be that as it may, I wish to point out that at the end of the day, what matters is that the message of the Latin oration is understood by the priest and communicated faithfully to the liturgical assembly. This imposes on any translator a good grasp of the medieval Latin used in the liturgy and the hermeneutical skill to interpret Latin liturgical texts.[4]

Needless to say, no liturgical text, be it in Latin or English, embodies everything there is to say about God and his marvelous deeds; and there is no liturgical translation that will perfectly and fully capture what is contained in the venerable corpus of Latin orations.

It is my hope that this small volume will be a companion to priests and faithful alike as they journey in liturgical worship along the (as yet) unfamiliar terrain of the new English translation. This volume aims to assist clergy and faithful to develop a deeper appreciation of the church's venerable corpus of liturgical orations and to offer a possible method of interpreting them.

My gratitude goes to Dean Josefina Manabat and Fr. Genaro Diwa. They equipped me with reading and research materials that made the work lighter. I also thank Mr. Peter Dwyer for the interest he manifested in this project and the useful suggestions he made regarding the approach to so delicate a topic as liturgical translation.

That in all things God may be glorified.

General Observations

The Orations

The Latin formularies, many of which date from the sixth century, are marked by the Roman euchological attribute consisting of brevity, sobriety, and the use of rhetorical devices such as the *cursus, concinnitas,* and parallelism. The older Collects consistently observe the classical structure of presidential prayers. These are invocation (O God), amplification of the invocation (O God, who . . .), petition (with imperative or subjunctive verb), motive for the petition, and conclusion.[5] The three types of orations, namely, the Collect, Prayer over the Offerings, and Prayer after Communion, conclude respectively the rite preceding them. While the Collects deal with theological and spiritual themes, the Prayers over the Offerings and the Prayers after Communion are linked by and large to the respective parts of the Mass. These allude to the mystery laid on the altar and received in Holy Communion.

Some of the Latin orations are literary masterpieces, exquisitely crafted. Their literary art and pleasing sound are often lost in translation, unless special effort is made to capture them through equivalent literary devices in the receptor language. The two Collects below (Thursday after Ash Wednesday and Seventh Sunday in Ordinary Time) are examples of classic Roman orations:

> Actiones nostras, quaesumus, Domine,
> aspirando praeveni et adiuvando prosequere,
> ut cuncta nostra operatio a te semper incipiat,
> et per te coepta finiatur.

> Praesta, quaesumus, omnipotens Deus,
> ut, semper rationabilia meditantes,
> quae tibi sunt placita, et dictis exsequamur et factis.

We should not confine our appreciation of the orations to their magnificent literary style. Each of them has a doctrine to communicate, a spiritual insight to share. For example, the orations in Advent enrich our understanding of this season as they invite us to meditate on its twofold character as a time of preparation for Christmas and of joyful expectation for the second coming. The collect for Monday of the First Week of Advent is one such example:

> Keep us alert, we pray, O Lord our God,
> as we await the advent of Christ your Son,
> so that, when he comes and knocks,
> he may find us watchful in prayer
> and exultant in his praise.

As a general observation, it can be said that the orations, especially the Collects, unfold the theology and spirituality of seasons and feasts in the course of the eucharistic celebration.

On the other hand, the orations in Ordinary Time, unlike those of the seasons and feasts, deal with broad theological and spiritual themes. There are several orations, however, that are theologically profound and spiritually uplifting. One example is a passage from the Prayer over the Offerings (Second Sunday): "whenever the memorial of this sacrifice is celebrated the work of our redemption is accomplished." A theologically loaded statement such as this is a rich source for homily and catechesis. Other orations urge us to live according to the theological virtues of faith, hope, and charity, or exhort us to put into practice the Christian moral values of repentance, forgiveness, and works of love. Typical of such orations is the Collect for the Thirtieth Sunday:

> Almighty ever-living God,
> increase our faith, hope and charity,
> and make us love what you command,
> so that we may merit what you promise.

Conclusions to the Orations

Through our Lord Jesus Christ, your Son,
who lives and reigns with you in the unity of the Holy Spirit,
one God, for ever and ever.

Who lives and reigns with you in the unity of the Holy Spirit,
one God, for ever and ever.

Through Christ our Lord.
Who lives and reigns for ever and ever.

Interpretation of the Texts

The first two conclusions are used for the Collect; the last two for the Prayer over the Offerings, Prayer after Communion, and Prayer over the People.

These four forms of conclusion to the orations do not have subject and verb. Their peculiar English construction can be explained by recourse to the Latin texts, which have no subject or verb either. They are a type of Latin ellipsis. Usage will determine whether ellipsis will work equally well in English as it does in Latin. The following orations are random examples. The first is the Collect for Wednesday during the Weekdays of Christmas Time. It is obvious that the concluding relative pronoun "Who" does not refer to "renewal" but to the "bringer of your salvation," which is a couple of lines away:

Grant us, almighty God, that the bringer of your salvation,
who for the world's redemption came forth with newness of
    heavenly light,
may dawn afresh in our hearts and bring us constant renewal.
Who lives and reigns with you in the unity of the Holy Spirit,
one God, for ever and ever.

The second example is the Collect for Friday during the First Week of Advent. Because of the proximity of "we" to "Who live and reign," those who listen to the oration might construe the plural noun "we" as the subject of the sentence, although the possibility would be rather distant if the priest observed the correct pause:

> Stir up your power, we pray, O Lord, and come,
> that with you to protect us,
> we may find rescue
> from the pressing dangers of our sins,
> and with you to set us free,
> we may be found worthy of salvation.
> Who live and reign with God the Father
> in the unity of the Holy Spirit,
> one God, for ever and ever.

The Latin conclusion is "Per Dominum nostrum Iesum Christum" (Through our Lord Jesus Christ), whose earlier version is the simple "Per Christum Dominum nostrum" (Through Christ our Lord). It is a fixed formulary that was appended to the main body of orations in medieval sacramentaries and served as a reminder that every prayer should appeal to Christ's mediation. Oftentimes, the conclusion is shortened to the preposition *Per* or *Per Dominum*. This is still observed in the current Missale Romanum. The early Latin orations had been originally composed without an explicit conclusion.

Although the conclusion appears as a separate unit, it is an integral part of the oration: it conveys Christ's mediation and reinforces the petition expressed by imperative verbs like *da, praesta, concede,* and *tribue.* Hence, though somewhat disconnected from the main body of the oration, "Per Christum Dominum nostrum" functions as the mediatory element of the petition.

In homily and catechesis it is important to make clear the connection between Christ's mediation and the petition. It helps to keep in mind that the conclusion is not a unit separate from the oration notwithstanding the word order and the ellipsis of the Latin formulary. In the liturgy prayers are normally addressed to God through Christ the Mediator.

By way of an example, the following restructuring of the Collect for the Twelfth Sunday in Ordinary Time can elucidate the connection:

Grant, O Lord,
that we may always revere and love your holy name,
for you never deprive of your guidance
those you set firm on the foundation of your love.
Through our Lord Jesus Christ, your Son,
who lives and reigns with you in the unity of the Holy Spirit,
one God, for ever and ever.

In the long form of the English conclusion, the adjective "one" is in-serted before "God." There is no *unus* (one) in the Latin original. Since the conclusion is trinitarian, the appendage of "one" seems to affirm the doctrine that the three Divine Persons are one God. This is of course theologically correct, but it is not what the Latin text is saying. *Deus* is in the vocative case and refers only to the Person addressed in the prayer.

> The sense of the long conclusion to the orations is "We beg you, O God (*Deus*), to grant our petition through our Lord Jesus Christ, your Son, who lives and reigns with you in the unity of the Holy Spirit, for ever and ever."

Homiletic-Catechetical Note

"Per Christum Dominum nostrum" translates into liturgical prayer the teaching of Christ that no one can come to the Father except through him (John 14:6). The prayer of the church is pleasing to God, because Jesus Christ, the Mediator, transports it to the throne of grace. Hence, in her prayers the church always invokes, explicitly or implicitly, Christ's role as Mediator.

It may be said that Christ owns the liturgical prayer that the church recites in his name, so that God beholds the countenance of the Son in the worshiping assembly. Because of the church's union with Christ, God answers her prayer as if it were the prayer of Christ himself. Ultimately, the efficacy of the church's prayer rests on Christ himself.[6]

"Per Christum Dominum nostrum" gives us the assurance that when we pray through Christ our Mediator, God is listening.

"We Pray"

Another preliminary observation is in reference to the insertion of the ubiquitous clause "we pray," which is the equivalent of the ever-present *quaesumus*. How important is quaesumus in Latin orations? It is believed to be one of the oldest elements of Roman orations in pre-Christian times. Christians inherited it and used it liberally in their Euchology. Quaesumus has two functions in classical orations. The first is to soften the commanding tone of imperative verbs such as *da* (give) and *praesta* (grant). The second is to enhance the rhythm of the oration. It is enclitic and, being unaccented, it contributes to the cadence of sentences that have strong accented verbs. Frequent examples are *da quaesumus, praesta quaesumus,* and *tribue quaesumus.*[7] Here is an example from the Collect for Friday in the Second Week of Lent:

> Da, quæsumus, omnipotens Deus,
> ut, sacro nos purificante pænitentiæ studio,
> sinceris mentibus ad sancta ventura facias pervenire.

There seems to be an overload of the enclitic "we pray" in the new English orations, but that is because there is a generous supply of quaesumus in the Latin formularies. It is attached, for purposes named above, to a good number of imperative verbs.

In some instances "we pray" is inserted in the middle of a sentence. This could disrupt the flow of the sentence. One example is the Collect for Friday after the Sixth Sunday of Easter:

> O God, who restore us to eternal life
> in the Resurrection of Christ,
> raise us up, we pray, to the author of our salvation,
> who is seated at your right hand . . .

Depending on how the priest makes the pause, the people in the assembly might hear "Raise us up; we pray to the author of salvation." Nonetheless, the clausal break, like a hump on the road, can be a useful device against speeding too quickly through the prayer.

One question, however, is whether the clause "we pray" has as much importance in English as "quaesumus" has in Latin? Will the frequent repetition of the same clause eventually cause tedium (the technical term is *repetita nauseant*)? To add to this, there are several orations in the new English Missal where the clause "we pray" is inserted even if the Latin formularies abstain from using quaesumus. Some random examples are Collect for Wednesday, Second Week of Advent; Collect for Tuesday, Third Week of Advent; Collect and Prayer after Communion for December 19; and Collect for the Nineteenth Sunday in Ordinary Time. Considering the countless times "quaesumus" appears in the Latin prayer formularies, the frequent repetition of "we pray" in order to remind us about the majesty of God should not overly weary us.

Sometimes quaesumus is not used in the Latin text as an enclitic but as the main verb. If it is translated as enclitic, a difficulty will arise regarding the sentence construction that can adversely affect its proclamation as oration. An example is the Prayer after Communion for the Memorial of Saint Charles Lwanga and Companions on June 3:

> We have received this divine Sacrament, O Lord,
> as we celebrate the victory of your holy Martyrs;
> may what helped them to endure torment, we pray,
> make us, in the face of trials,
> steadfast in faith and in charity.

In the Latin text of the above prayer, quaesumus is the main verb followed by the *ut* clause. If it is so translated, the prayer is easier to read and to follow:

> We have received this divine Sacrament, O Lord,
> as we celebrate the victory of your holy Martyrs;
> we pray that what helped them to endure torment
> may make us, in the face of trials,
> steadfast in faith and in charity.

The Latin orations have a decidedly great predilection for quaesumus. However, in Latin there are alternative ways to say the same thing. Examples are *concede propitius*, *operare placatus*, and *supplices te rogamus*. They give us a wide margin to be creative in the translation of quaesumus.

Moreover, some English imperative verbs, like "grant," imply acknowledgment of both God's superiority and our humble condition. Depending on the context of the oration, "grant" does not require toning down as in the following petitions: "Lamb of God, you take away the sins of the world, grant us peace" and "Eternal rest grant unto them, O Lord."

A lexical analysis of the verb *quaeso* leads us to infer that the generic clause "we pray" falls short of fully expressing the nuance of quaesumus that is aptly conveyed in English by "we entreat," "we implore," or "we beseech." However, the oft-repeated "we pray" serves the purpose of reminding us during prayer that we are unworthy human beings in the presence of God's majesty.

Mystery/Mysteries

A word that recurs with frequency in the orations is "mysteries." In our day, when the word can signify a variety of things, it is necessary to explain what it denotes and connotes in the Latin and, consequently, English orations.[8]

The first thing to remember is that "mysteries" and "mystery" are often interchanged. As a whole, there is no difference in meaning between one and the other. "The plural can, of course, be explained by the general rule according to which the names of feasts, rites, etc., are used in the plural. Hence, too, it is by far the more frequently used. The singular seems to be somewhat more vague and means 'the sacramental action' in a rather general way; while the plural seems to be more concrete, and regards the sacramental rites as here and now in progress."[9]

Another thing to bear in mind when dealing with the meaning of mystery or mysteries is that the word has different meanings or connotations depending on the context. The context is the type of oration (Collect, Prayer over the Offerings, or Prayer after Communion) in which it is used. Another context to consider is the theme of the feast or the season. There is no hard-and-fast rule for determining the precise meaning of the word.

Mystery can denote the revealed truth of faith. This is quite obvious in the Collect of the Most Holy Trinity, where *admirabile mysterium* (wondrous mystery) refers to the doctrine of the holy Trinity:

> God our Father, who, by sending into the world
> the Word of truth and the Spirit of sanctification,
> made known to the human race your wondrous mystery,
> grant us, we pray, that in professing the true faith
> we may acknowledge the Trinity of eternal glory
> and adore your Unity, powerful in majesty.

Similarly, the plural *sacra mysteria* (sacred mysteries) in the Collect of Corpus Christi points to the presence of Christ's Body and Blood in the sacrament as a doctrine of faith:

> O God, who in this wonderful Sacrament
> have left us a memorial of your Passion,
> grant us, we pray,
> so to revere the sacred mysteries of your Body and Blood
> that we may always experience in ourselves
> the fruits of your redemption.

It is significant to note that these feasts of the Holy Trinity and Corpus Christi are strongly doctrinal in origin and euchological formulation.

More frequently, mystery signifies the sacrament of the Eucharist. In Prayers after Communion sacred mysteries, heavenly mysteries, and eternal mysteries refer to the Body and Blood of Christ. As a rule of thumb, one may safely interpret mystery or sacrament in the Prayers after Communion to mean eucharistic communion. A typical example is the Prayer after Communion on Thursday after the Third Sunday of Easter. In this and similar instances, "heavenly mysteries" is best interpreted as "heavenly sacrament":

> Graciously be present to your people, we pray, O Lord,
> and lead those you have imbued with heavenly mysteries
> to pass from former ways to newness of life.

The third meaning of mystery or mysteries is the liturgical celebration of the Eucharist. On several occasions the word "sacrament" substitutes "mystery." Generally, they mean the same thing. For example, in the Collect for Corpus Christi "wonderful Sacrament" (*sacramento mirabili*) stands for the eucharistic celebration, which is the memorial of Christ's passion.

However, this particular meaning is not always evident and may require us to take a closer look at the text. Such, for example, is the word "mysteries" in the Collect for the night of Christmas:

> O God, who have made this most sacred night
> radiant with the splendor of the true light,
> grant, we pray, that we, who have known the mysteries of his light
>   on earth,
> may also delight in his gladness in heaven.

"Mysteries" here is ambiguous. It can refer to the revealed truth about Christ's descent on earth (mystery of his light) as well as to the liturgical rite with which we commemorate his birth.

There is at least one occasion, in the Prayer after Communion (Thirty-Fourth Week in Ordinary Time), when the English oration qualifies *divina participatione* (divine participation) with the word "mysteries": "you give the joy of participating in divine mysteries." In general, participating in divine mysteries means taking part in the liturgical rite. However, what the Latin text suggests is sharing in the divine life or receiving the sacrament of the Eucharist.

Interpreting *mysterium* and *mysteria* every time they appear in the Latin orations is a daunting challenge to translators. Do they refer to an article of faith, to the sacrament of Christ's Body and Blood, or to the celebration of the liturgy? Perhaps it is a sensible decision to translate these elusive words simply as mystery or mysteries as they appear in Latin and commit to priests and catechists the responsibility of interpreting them.

Upper- and Lowercases

In the new English Roman Missal a good number of nouns are in initial capital letters, in contrast with the current English system. Examples abound: Eucharistic Bread and Chalice; Incarnation, Passion, Death, Ascension, and Resurrection of Christ; Sacraments, whether generic or particular; Cross and Resurrection; Paschal Mystery; Kingdom of God; Bishops, Priests, and Deacons; and many more. The frequent use of the uppercase is presumably intended to reinforce the sacral character of English in the liturgy.

The Latin Missal is sparing in its use of initial capital letters. They are reserved to the Body and Blood of Christ, the Angels and Saints, and a few others. In several instances, when English words are in the uppercase, the Latin is in the lower: *panis* and *calix* (eucharistic); *crux, mors,* and *resurrectio* (of Christ); *paschale mysterium; episcopus* (except when names of bishops are mentioned in the eucharistic prayer).

Initial capital letters do not, of course, concern the liturgical assembly, since they do not see the printed text, but they do affect the interpretation of the word or phrase.

An example is the Collect for Monday within the Octave of Easter. The English translation has "Sacrament" where the Latin has *sacramentum:*

> O God, who give constant increase
> to your Church by new offspring,
> grant that your servants may hold fast in their lives
> to the Sacrament they have received in faith.

To what does Sacrament refer? Among Catholic faithful, it commonly indicates the Blessed Sacrament. In the Latin corpus of Collects, *sacramentum* or *sacramenta,* like *mysterium* or *mysteria,* signifies almost always the liturgical rite. In the Prayers over the Gifts and Prayers after Communion, they designate the Eucharist or even Holy Communion. In the Collect above, however, Sacrament does not mean the Eucharist, Blessed Sacrament, or the liturgical rite. Taking into account the context of the oration, we should read it as the sacrament of baptism or, more precisely in the light of the church's older tradition, the sacraments of Christian initiation.

It is useful to know that the orations in the octave of Easter focus our attention on the neophytes, the sacrament of baptism, and the growth of the Christian people. In fact, the sacraments of Christian initiation and their effects like rebirth and future resurrection are the themes the majority of the orations address at this time. Thus, the "paschal mysteries" in the Prayer after Communion of Easter Sunday means the sacraments of initiation:

> Look upon your Church, O God,
> with unfailing love and favor,
> so that, renewed by the paschal mysteries,
> she may come to the glory of the resurrection.

A second example of the use of the uppercase that needs to be probed is the Collect for Friday within the same octave. The English has "Paschal Mystery," while the Latin, *paschale sacramentum*. First of all, this oration does not say *paschale mysterium*. This is probably one of the infrequent cases in the Roman Missal when mystery and sacrament are not interchangeable. Again, taken in context, "Paschal Mystery" refers to the sacraments of Christian initiation, not to the paschal mystery of Christ's death and resurrection:

> Almighty ever-living God,
> who gave us the Paschal Mystery
> in the covenant you established
> for reconciling the human race,
> so dispose our minds, we pray,
> that what we celebrate by professing the faith
> we may express in deeds.

The following literal translation can help us grasp more easily the sense of the Collect:

> Almighty ever-living God,
> who provided the paschal sacrament
> in the covenant of human reconciliation,
> give us to understand that what we celebrate by faith
> we should imitate by deeds.

Advent

Prayer over the Offerings
Wednesday, First Week of Advent

> May the sacrifice of our worship, Lord, we pray,
> be offered to you unceasingly,
> to complete what was begun in sacred mystery
> and powerfully accomplish for us your saving work.

> to complete what was begun in sacred mystery

Interpretation of the Text

The line "to complete what was begun in sacred mystery" is difficult in both the new English translation and the Latin original. What is sacred mystery, what was begun in it, and how will it be completed? Recourse to the Latin text can shed some light on this obscure passage: "Hostia immoletur, quae sacri peragat instituta mysterii." In classical Latin the verb *peragat* means "to complete," but in medieval liturgical Latin it means "to celebrate." *Devotio* is self-dedication with cultic connotation; it is the sacred action that takes place at the altar.[10] *Instituta* is institution. In this particular oration, it refers to the institution of the sacred mystery, which is the Eucharist.[11] Thus, we should interpret the oration as saying that the offering of the sacrifice on the altar celebrates and recalls the Last Supper. Below is a literal translation of this prayer:

> May the sacrifice of our dedication to you,
> we pray, O Lord, be offered unceasingly,
> for it celebrates the institution of the sacred mystery
> and powerfully enacts for us your salvation.

> The sense of this Prayer over the Offerings is "May the sacrifice of our dedication to God, which celebrates the institution of the sacred mystery and brings about our salvation, be offered to him unceasingly."

Homiletic-Catechetical Note

This prayer sums up in one short sentence the well-known relationship between sacrifice and meal, between Calvary and Cenacle. The Eucharist we celebrate is the presence "in mystery" of the sacrifice that Christ offered once for all upon the altar of Calvary. At Holy Mass that presence "in mystery" takes the form of a ritual meal. We are transported to the event of the Last Supper when, in anticipation of his death on the cross, Christ broke the bread.

What is so striking about the prayer is its theological twist: the sacrifice of Christ, which we offer "in mystery" on the altar, celebrates the meal in the Cenacle and perpetuates it. Normally we say that the meal aspect of the Eucharist brings us back to the cross, that the external rite of Holy Mass veils the event of Christ's sacrifice. But now this prayer teaches us that it also works the other way around. The sacrifice we offer is our supper with the Lord Jesus. What we have on the altar is the sacrifice of his Body and Blood that reminds us of the bread he broke and the chalice he passed around to his disciples.

When we gaze on the table in the sanctuary, we perceive in faith the altar of the cross that was planted on Calvary. When we partake of the consecrated bread and wine, we eat and drink from the altar of sacrifice. The church is Cenacle and within it is Calvary. The Eucharist is the sacrifice of the cross and it actualizes, extending to our time, the night when Christ ate his Last Supper with his disciples.

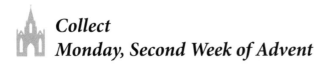

Collect
Monday, Second Week of Advent

May our prayer of petition
rise before you, we pray, O Lord,
that, with purity unblemished,
we, your servants, may come, as we desire,
to celebrate the great mystery
of the Incarnation of your Only Begotten Son.

> we, your servants, may come, as we desire,
> / to celebrate

Interpretation of the Text

Some passages in this Collect require closer attention. What is the meaning of "we . . . may come, as we desire"? Depending on how it is read, it can be interpreted in two ways: it is our desire to come, or we may come at will. However, the comma after the clause makes the sense sufficiently clear. At any rate, "as we desire" and "to celebrate" are not in the Latin original, but they help us understand the prayer. Furthermore, "we, your servants," which is not a literal translation, is a good dynamic equivalent of *nostrae vota servitutis* (literally, the vow of our servitude). It is helpful to note that the verbal phrase "we . . . may come" (the Latin is *pervenire*) carries the sense of "we may come to the knowledge" of the mystery of the incarnation.

The Latin sentence stripped down to its constitutive words reads "vota nostrae servitutis ad mysterium incarnationis perveniant" (May the vow of our servitude attain to the mystery of the incarnation). In fairness to the 2010 English translation, we should admit that the Latin text is not simple to translate literally without sounding awkward or even unintelligible. This probably explains why in this English version of the Collect recourse was appropriately made to dynamic translation. The following is a literal translation of the Collect:

> May the prayer of our petition, we pray,
> be directed in your sight, O Lord,
> that with pristine purity our perfect submission may attain
> to the great mystery of the incarnation of your Only Begotten.

> The sense of the Collect is "By our act of perfect submission to God, may we come to the knowledge of the mystery of the incarnation."

Homiletic-Catechetical Note

The Collect calls the incarnation of Christ a great mystery. The Constitution on the Sacred Liturgy of Vatican II and the postconciliar reform fittingly underscored the primacy of the paschal mystery in liturgical celebrations. After all, the resurrection of Christ is the kernel of our faith. However, we should not lose sight of the great mystery of the incarnation. In a sense, it was the most staggering, mind-boggling act of God. If we can believe that God became fully human, excepting sin, while remaining fully divine, we can believe that God suffered, died, and rose from the dead. The incarnation is the first stumbling block on the path of Christian faith.

At Easter time we stand to sing Alleluias of praise and thanksgiving to God because Christ is risen from the dead. Ancient Christian writers instructed the faithful not to kneel on Sunday; to do so was considered tantamount to a denial of the resurrection. But at Christmas time we kneel in front of the crib, while we recite the awe-inspiring statement of faith: "by the Holy Spirit [he] was incarnate of the Virgin Mary, and became man." We kneel before God who became humble as a helpless little child sleeping in the manger. What our eyes behold, our intellects cannot fathom. And so, we kneel in deep humility and in perfect submission of our minds to God's inscrutable design of becoming a human being. When the clarity of our reason acquiesces to the darkness of faith, we gain intimation, even if opaque and murky, of the great mystery of the incarnation.

Collect
December 18

Grant, we pray, almighty God,
that we, who are weighed down from of old
by slavery beneath the yoke of sin,
may be set free by the newness
of the long-awaited Nativity
of your Only Begotten Son.

> the newness / of the long-awaited Nativity

Interpretation of the Text

The Latin text is quite intricate. The method of formal correspondence does not work well for *nova nativitate*. Below is an attempt to translate it using both methods of formal correspondence and dynamic equivalence:

Grant, we pray, almighty God,
that we, who are bowed down by the yoke of sin
caused by ancient slavery,
may be set free by the awaited new birth
of your only Begotten.

In this literal translation the meaning of "new birth" still remains as vague as the Latin *nova nativitate*. The 2010 version renders it as "the newness / of the long-awaited Nativity / of your Only Begotten Son."

To interpret "newness of the . . . Nativity," it is useful to refer to the literary style of the Latin Collect, which employs the rhetorical device known as antithesis or juxtaposition of contrasting concepts: "vetusta servitute deprimimur; nova nativitate liberemur" (we are weighed down by the old servitude; we are freed by the new birth). *Vetustas* is the condition of unredeemed humanity: "The state of sin is represented as old in contrast to the newness of life brought by Christ."[12] The adjectives *vetusta* (old or ancient) and *nova* (new) can be conveniently interpreted in a temporal, adverbial sense. For purposes of translation, it is useful to note that in Latin, adjectives can have the function of adverbs and substantives.

> The sense of the Collect is "We, who in former times have been weighed down by enslavement to sin, are in these latter days set free by the birth of Christ."

Homiletic-Catechetical Note

The birth of Christ ushered in a new age marked by freedom from the oppressive dominion of sin. When he appeared in human flesh, he contested the power of evil over human beings and restored the original image in which they had been created. Because he took to himself our human body, soul, heart, mind, and spirit, he has made us once again the vessel of God's holiness. Even if, God forbid, our vessel of clay should break, we have the assurance that the Divine Potter can restore the pristine beauty and integrity of our being and repair our fractured vessel of clay. The former times spelled despair; the latter days launched new hope.

God's design to save humankind after the fall of our first parents had lain hidden in his eternal heart. But the birth of Christ in these last days revealed it. God's plan received at last a human face. The promise was fulfilled. We speak no longer of former times but of the latter days when the Word was made flesh and dwelt among us.

We gather from the Collect that Christ has brought the world to the end of the ages. He has completed everything in God's plan. "It is finished"; the day's work is done. Evening and night have descended, and now we long for the dawning of the eternal day. Tomorrow, at break of that new day, we shall behold the glory of the incarnate Word. Meanwhile, we sit in the darkness of faith waiting for the final revelation of Christ.

Fulfillment means that there is conclusiveness in God's plan. Christ was born in our time once for all, just as he died and rose from the dead once for all. He will not be born again, because he does not regret what he accomplished by his birth. But the church will continue until the end of time to remember and celebrate the great mystery of the incarnation. This is the newness referred to by the Collect.

Christmas Time

Prayer over the Offerings
Vigil Mass, The Nativity of the Lord

As we look forward, O Lord,
to the coming festivities,
may we serve you all the more eagerly
for knowing that in them
you make manifest the beginnings of our redemption.

---

for knowing that in them / you make manifest

Interpretation of the Text

The passage "for knowing that in them / you make manifest" requires some explaining. Perhaps it will read better without the conjunction "for." At any rate, it is helpful to consult the Latin oration.

In liturgical Latin, *sollemnia* carries different meanings, depending on the context. It can denote yearly celebration, the liturgical action itself, or the feast. Here it refers to the annual feast of Christmas.[13] It is in the plural form, but like other substantives in the plural, it is correct to treat it as a singular noun. In the context of the Prayer over the Offerings, the word "service" (*servitium*) evokes liturgical service.[14] The Latin text employs the binary *tanto-quanto*, thereby expressing the urgent or pressing need to get ready for the approaching feast of Christ's birth. Hence, to explain the sense of the English text, it is useful to keep in mind that "festivities" refers to Christmas and "serve" to our participation in the liturgical rite. The following is a literal translation of the prayer:

Grant, we pray, O Lord,
that with a more eager act of service

we may hasten to the solemn feast,
the more so as in it
you show the beginning of our redemption.

> The sense of the Prayer over the Offerings is "By participating more eagerly in the liturgy, may we hasten to the approaching feast of the Nativity, by which you reveal the beginning of our redemption."

Homiletic-Catechetical Note

In the feast of Christ's birth we see the beginning of our salvation. The oration does not say "in Christ's birth" but in the liturgical celebration of it. This might sound somehow perplexing, since the beginning of salvation is verified in the historical event of Christ's birth rather than in its subsequent liturgical commemoration. The difficulty disappears, if we keep in mind that in the liturgy the mystery of Christ is recalled through what liturgists call *anamnesis* or ritual memorial.

In virtue of this action of the church, the mystery that is commemorated becomes present to the assembly by the power of the Holy Spirit. The Constitution on the Sacred Liturgy sheds light on this: "Thus recalling the mysteries of the redemption, [the church] opens up to the faithful the riches of the Lord's powers and merits, so that these are in some way made present at all times; the faithful lay hold of them and are filled with saving grace" (102).[15]

When we celebrate the birth of Christ, we do not merely call to mind the night when he was born. We are, as it were, transported to the event in Bethlehem, or, better yet, the event is made present to us in the Eucharist we celebrate. The Prayer over the Offerings teaches us that in the Eucharist the mystery becomes as large as life. With our eyes of faith we gaze on what Mary and the shepherds beheld. Liturgists call this "presence in mystery."

When we participate actively and devoutly in the liturgy, we enter into the *sollemnia*, the mystery of Christ's birth, made present in the celebration. We lay hold of it and are filled with saving grace.

Collect
Mass during the Day, The Nativity of the Lord

O God, who wonderfully created the dignity of human nature
and still more wonderfully restored it,
grant, we pray,
that we may share in the divinity of Christ,
who humbled himself to share in our humanity.

> who humbled himself to share in our humanity

Interpretation of the Text

The incarnation is the mystery of God's descent among us to share in the nature of human creatures. It was God's awesome act of self-humiliation. This must have been the thinking behind the English translation "who humbled himself to share in our humanity."

The Collect, however, uses a carefully chosen verb to signify Christ's pleasure and goodwill toward the human race when he became incarnate. The verb is *dignatus est* (he was pleased; he considered it worthy), not *semetipsum humiliavit* (he humbled himself).[16] The English Collect for the Holy Family translates *dignatus es* (*es* is the second-person singular of *esse*, to be; *est* is the third-person singular) in the former, not latter, sense of the word: "O God, who were pleased to give us . . . ."

Commentators on this Collect are of the opinion that it was penned by Pope Leo the Great to counter the Manicheans of his time who disparaged the dignity of human nature.[17] He argued that the incarnation was God's recognition of the human dignity he had created. The words *dignitatem* and *dignatus est* are closely related to each other. They tell us that

God had created the human dignity and was pleased to restore it back to its noble condition after it had been infected by sin. The following is a literal translation of the Collect:

> O God, who created wonderfully the dignity of the human nature
> but more wonderfully restored it,
> grant to us, we pray, to be sharers in the divinity of him
> who was pleased to become a partaker in our humanity.

> The sense of the Collect is "Even if human dignity had been marred by sin, Christ considered it still worthy of his incarnation."

Homiletic-Catechetical Note

The Collect is a timely reminder of the inalienable dignity of every human person. The torrent of sin is not able to wipe it out. Every person, saint or sinner, woman or man, child or adult deserves respect because of the innate dignity bestowed by the Creator and confirmed by the incarnate Savior who acknowledged it and assumed it unto himself. God was not ashamed of the abased condition of humans after sin had been committed.

The homily of Pope Leo the Great on the Nativity of the Lord is at once magnificent, memorable, and moving. It is the Collect of Christmas Day in homiletic form:

> Christian, remember your dignity, and now that you share in God's own nature, do not return by sin to your former base condition. Bear in mind who is your head and of whose body you are a member. Do not forget that you have been rescued from the power of darkness and brought into the light of God's kingdom.
>
> Through the sacrament of baptism you have become a temple of the Holy Spirit. Do not drive away so great a guest by evil conduct and become again a slave to the devil, for your liberty was bought by the blood of Christ.

Collect
December 30

Grant, we pray, almighty God,
that the newness of the Nativity in the flesh
of your Only Begotten Son may set us free,
for ancient servitude holds us bound
beneath the yoke of sin.

> the newness of the Nativity in the flesh

Interpretation of the Text

Nova nativitas/vetusta servitus (new birth/old slavery) appears also
in the Latin Collect of December 18. Both Collects say practically the
same thing, except that in the Collect under consideration *nova* has the
sense of present occurrence: it takes place today. We hold the solemn
memorial of Christ's Nativity today.

The liturgical form our celebration of Christ's Nativity takes is the
Eucharist. In it we celebrate a liturgical mystery rather than commemorate
a historical event. It is divine reality, present and active, allowing us to
lay hold of it and be filled with saving grace (cf. Constitution on the Sacred
Liturgy 102). The petition that Christ's Nativity "may set us free" is to be
read in the context of the mysterious presence of Christ's birth in the
eucharistic celebration. Below is a literal translation of the Collect:

Grant, we pray, almighty God,
that the Nativity in the flesh today
of your Only Begotten

may free us,
whom past slavery held bound
under the yoke of sin.

> The sense of the Collect is "The Nativity of Christ, which we celebrate today in the liturgy of Christmas, is mysteriously present in the liturgical rites and prayers, setting us free from the slavery of sin."

Homiletic-Catechetical Note

In the liturgy we often come across the word *hodie*, today. It gives the sensation that what is celebrated is taking place today. The liturgy breaches the wall that divides past and present, history and mystery. Through rites and prayers (*per ritus et preces*) we call on God to come and be present; we invoke the Holy Spirit to bring into our midst the mystery of Christ that we celebrate. Today Christ is born unto us; today he endured the pain of Calvary; today he rose from the dead; today he ascended into heaven; and today he sent down the Holy Spirit.

The word *nova* in the Collect is another way of saying that when we celebrate the birth of Christ today, this mystery of faith, this mystery of his incarnation, is at hand. We are unable to return to the past, but by the power of the Holy Spirit the past breaks into our historical time; it inserts itself in our midst. Indeed, in the liturgy we witness the past events of salvation history and are given the privilege to enjoy a foretaste of what awaits us. In the liturgy everything happens today.

Collect
Solemnity of Mary, Mother of God, January 1

O God, who through the fruitful virginity of Blessed Mary
bestowed on the human race
the grace of eternal salvation,
grant, we pray,
that we may experience the intercession of her,
through whom we were found worthy
to receive the author of life,
our Lord Jesus Christ, your Son.

> through whom we were found worthy / to receive
> the author of life

Interpretation of the Text

The role of Mary in salvation history as Mother of God and Mother of the church should not be played down in our theological thinking, but neither should it be the object of pious exaggerations. Good theology requires balance and moderation. Such are the qualities we find in liturgical orations that talk about Mary.

How should we understand the English translation "through whom [Mary] we were found worthy / to receive the author of life"? Will we not raise a theological dispute if we affirm that through Mary we were found worthy to receive Christ? Perhaps a better question to ask is how to translate the Latin text without causing unnecessary doctrinal concern.

The Latin oration reads, "per quam meruimus Filium tuum auctorem vitae suscipere." The crux of interpretation is the phrase *meruimus*

suscipere. "There is the oft-recurring use of certain periphrastic constructions. One such is the formation with *mereri*. Of the 45 times that this
verb occurs in the orations, only four have the meaning of 'to merit' in
the strict sense of the word. In the rest it is a term of reverence which
implies the reception of a 'free gift' for which one depends entirely on the
benign favor of God."[18] *Mereri* is used as a rhetorical device to underline
the attitude of reverence during prayer. Periphrastic constructions, like
mereri suscipere, work very well in Latin classical orations, but they are
seldom, if at all, translated. In this particular Collect it is best to ignore
it or substitute it with a word that expresses the sentiment of gratitude
and respect.

Thus, the passage "through whom [Mary] we were found worthy"
might be affirming more than what the Latin text is saying. When we
explain it, we need to caution ourselves that it is only through Christ the
Mediator that God had found us worthy. The notion of being worthy
before God springs, not from Mary's intercession, but from the sacrifice
of reconciliation that Christ has accomplished for us. The following is a
literal translation of the Collect:

> O God, who bestowed on the human race,
> by the fruitful virginity of Blessed Mary,
> the rewards of eternal salvation,
> grant us, we pray, to feel the intercession of her
> through whom we have undeservedly received
> your Son, the author of life.

> The sense of the Collect is "Through Mary, fruitful
> virgin, God gave to the world the reward of eternal
> life, Jesus Christ himself; through her virginal
> motherhood we have received, unworthy though
> we were, the author of life."

Homiletic-Catechetical Note

When Christmas received an octave in the seventh century, the Roman
Church placed on the octave day itself the *Natale S. Mariae*, which hon-

ored Mary as the Mother of God. The feast existed in the Eastern churches already in the fifth century, a little before the Council of Ephesus (431), which defined Mary as *Theotokos*, Mother of God. It is the oldest feast of Mary in the Roman Church.

The octave of Christmas, which is also New Year's Day and the World Day of Peace, is above all the feast of Mary, Mother of God. It is significant that the church opens the cycle of the year invoking the Mother of God who is also Mother of the church. What does this mean? It means that Mary is also the mother of Jesus' sisters and brothers. Before he died on the cross, he entrusted us to the care of his mother. He said to the Beloved Disciple that represented us at the foot of the cross, "Behold, your mother." And to her he said, "Woman, behold, your son." From that time on, anyone who believed in Jesus became daughter or son of his mother.

When we traverse the year with all its changes and chances, we put our trust in the motherly care of Mary. She will be attentive to us, as she was attentive to her Son Jesus. When trials afflict us, she will keep her post by our side. When we are lost, she will search for us, as she did when the Child Jesus was lost in Jerusalem. When we undergo agony in the garden and carry the cross, she will not be far away to give us comfort and courage. That is the kind of mother we have in Mary.

The magnificent and inspiring Memorare prayer, with roots at least to the fifteenth century, expands the theme of the Collect: "Remember, O most gracious Virgin Mary, that never was it known that anyone who fled to your protection, implored your help, or sought your intercession was left unaided. Inspired with this confidence, I fly unto you, O Virgin of virgins, my Mother. To you I come, before you I stand, sinful and sorrowful. O Mother of the Word Incarnate, despise not my petitions, but in your mercy hear and answer me."

Lent

Collect
Ash Wednesday

Grant, O Lord, that we may begin with holy fasting
this campaign of Christian service,
so that, as we take up battle against spiritual evils,
we may be armed with weapons of self-restraint.

> this campaign of Christian service

Interpretation of the Text

The phrase "campaign of Christian service" illustrates the character of the Lenten season. But what does it mean? Campaign has a wide range of meaning from political action and military operation to crusades and advocacies. The Latin phrase is *praesidia militiae christianae*. *Praesidium* was a military defense or a garrison. Since training was carried out in it, its transferred meaning includes military exercises or discipline.[19] The connection between *praesidia* and campaign is difficult to establish.[20] In fact, the equivalent of campaign in classical Latin is *stipendium*, not *praesidia*. *Militia*, on the other hand, means military service or warfare. The Latin Collect adopts these military concepts and endows them with Lenten character. The phrase "Christian service" is generic, but in this Collect it possesses the nuance of *militia*. It means Christian warfare. Below is a literal translation of the Collect:

Grant us, O Lord, to begin with holy fasting
the exercises for Christian warfare,
that, as we do battle against spiritual evils,
we may be armed with the aid of self-discipline.

> The sense of the Collect is "We begin the exercises
> of Christian warfare with fasting, so that we may
> be armed with self-discipline when we do battle
> against the forces of evil."

Homiletic-Catechetical Note

The notion of Christian warfare is supported by Ephesians 6:14 ("stand fast . . . with righteousness as a breastplate") and 2 Corinthians 6:7 ("with weapons of righteousness at the right and at the left"). The sixth-century Rule of St. Benedict echoes this in its exhortation that monks should be "armed with the strong and noble weapons of obedience to do battle for the true King, Christ the Lord" (Prol. 3).[21]

Christian life is an incessant battle against evil. The traditional weapons are fasting, prayer, and almsgiving. They characterize the season of Lent. In this outlook the entire life of Christians is marked by the Lenten discipline of self-denial and works of charity. We read in the Rule of St. Benedict that "the life of a monk ought to be a continuous Lent. Since few, however, have the strength for this, we urge the entire community during these days of Lent to keep its manner of life most pure and to wash away in this holy season the negligences of other times" (49.1-3).

The Collect should thus be read in the broader context of our lifelong struggle against evil. Lent symbolizes that struggle; it is the training ground for Christian warfare. The gospel of the temptation of Christ in the desert where he fasted and prayed for forty days is a portrayal of the Lenten observance of Christians.

The discipline of Lent, such as fasting or sharing of one's resources with the poor, is designed to instill in us the virtues we need in order to do battle for Christ and to establish them as a permanent way of life.

Collect
First Sunday of Lent

Grant, almighty God,
through the yearly observances of holy Lent,
that we may grow in understanding
of the riches hidden in Christ
and by worthy conduct pursue their effects.

> 1. Grant . . . through the yearly observances of
>   holy Lent, / that we may grow
> 2. the yearly observances of holy Lent

Interpretation of the Text

The positioning of the conjunction "that" (*ut* clause) affects the theological premise of the oration. The Latin text reads, "Grant that we may
grow through the observance of Lent." It does not say, "Grant through
the observance of Lent that we may grow." Our Lenten observance is not
God's motive for granting our prayer; rather, it is our instrument of
growth. To explain the sense of this English translation, it is necessary to
observe the Latin word order and move the conjunction "that" ahead of
the preceding phrase.

Conversatio allows for different interpretations.[22] In the context of
Lent as a season of spiritual renewal, it is fittingly rendered in English
as "conversion." In the Rule of St. Benedict (chap. 58) *conversatio morum*
(conversion of life) is one of the three vows of monastic profession.
Hence, the sense of the English Collect should be understood in this
manner:

> Grant, almighty God,
> that through the yearly observance of holy Lent
> we may grow in the understanding of the hidden riches of Christ
> and pursue its effects by a worthy conversion of life.

Now, how should the phrase "observances of holy Lent" be interpreted? The Latin is "annua quadragesimalis exercitia sacramenti" (literally, yearly exercises of the forty-day sacrament).[23] The "forty-day sacrament" can be rendered quite simply as "Lenten sacrament," which is how we are to interpret the phrase "holy Lent." In this Collect "holy" stands for the substantive *sacramenti* to which is attached the adjective *quadragesimalis*. But what does sacrament mean in this particular context?

The Latin oration, which is taken from the eighth-century Gelasian Sacramentary,[24] belongs to the corpus of prayers for the Stational Papal Masses during Lent.[25] These Lenten Masses were the eminent activities of the Roman Church as it prepared for the Easter feast. *Sacramentum* referred to these Masses and *exercitia* to the community's attendance for forty days. In short, the observances of Lent were the celebrations of the Eucharist for forty days prior to Easter and the faithful's participation in them.

"The riches hidden in Christ" translates *Christi arcanum*. For a fuller understanding of "the riches hidden in Christ," it helps to remember that *arcanum* "refers not only to the mystery of Christ, but also to the rites by which we participate in Christ's mystery."[26] The mystery of Christ, whose core is his death and resurrection, is none other than the paschal mystery. The liturgical rite by which the paschal mystery is celebrated is also called mystery.

> The sense of the Collect is "Through our annual forty-day participation in the celebration of the liturgy, particularly the Holy Mass, may we grow in the understanding of Christ's paschal mystery."

Homiletic-Catechetical Note

At the start of the Lenten season the church calls on its members to spend more time in prayer, especially by taking part in the stational liturgy. Originally the Roman Lenten observance focused on the reading of God's word, whereby catechumens were instructed and the faithful were renewed in their faith as they prepared for the paschal sacraments. By the middle of the sixth century Rome's Lenten liturgy became eucharistic.[27]

This development has a significant impact on the way the faithful prepared for Easter. The Collect makes us understand that frequent, if not daily, participation in the Eucharist should be the prominent observance of Lenten discipline. Obviously, such participation becomes more meaningful when accompanied by daily conversion through daily meditation on the word of God and acts of justice and charity.

When the faithful take part frequently and devoutly in the celebration of Holy Mass, they gain a deeper insight on the paschal mystery, which is the heart of the eucharistic liturgy. The prayers, readings, and homiletic instruction unfold the meaning of Christ's mystery and the faithful are enabled to lay hold on it and be filled with its saving grace. In this sense, Lent is not merely a preparation for Easter; it represents the continuing effect of Christ's paschal mystery in the course of the liturgical year. Rightly, the entire life of a Christian is a Lenten observance marked by the Eucharist and works of love.

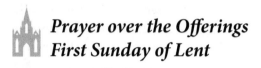 *Prayer over the Offerings*
First Sunday of Lent

Give us the right dispositions, O Lord, we pray,
to make these offerings,
for with them we celebrate the beginning
of this venerable and sacred time.

> we celebrate the beginning / of this venerable and
> sacred time

Interpretation of the Text

There is a profound doctrine concealed in the English version of this oration. What is meant by the statement, "we celebrate the beginning / of this venerable and sacred time"? To unravel it, we need to consult the Latin text: "ipsius venerabilis sacramenti celebramus exordium."

In liturgical lexicon *sacramentum* is almost always synonymous with *mysterium*, whose immediate meaning is the liturgical mystery or the paschal mystery itself.[28] In the context of the Prayer over the Offerings, the meaning of *sacramentum* is clearer, if it is translated as mystery rather than time. As a matter of fact, it is unusual for *sacramentum* to be translated as "time." Thus, we should understand the phrase "sacred time" as the paschal mystery, whose celebration is ushered in by Lent. Below is a literal translation of the Latin text:

Make us, we pray, O Lord,
to be properly disposed to offer these gifts,
by which we solemnize the start
of this revered mystery.

The season of Lent opens with the eucharistic celebration in which the paschal mystery is actualized. The prayer tells us that the celebration of Christ's death and resurrection starts with the Lenten season and progresses until it reaches its culmination in the great feast of Easter. In a word, the eucharistic gifts we offer at the beginning of Lent solemnly mark the start of the paschal season.

What is the meaning of the passage, "Give us the right dispositions . . . to make these offerings"? The Latin text can mean "enable us to offer these gifts properly" or "make our lives match the holiness of our gifts." Although the latter meaning is closer to the general tenor of Prayers over the Offerings, the former is equally important for a fuller appreciation of the prayer.[29]

> The sense of the Prayer over the Offerings is "Make our lives harmonize with the gifts we offer, for by them we commence the celebration of Christ's paschal mystery."

Homiletic-Catechetical Note

Lent is a journey toward the cross on Calvary and the empty tomb. All throughout this season the biblical readings at Mass instruct the faithful to accompany Christ as he directs his steps to the Jerusalem of his passion and death. They give in stages a glimpse of the paschal mystery. For example, the gospel of the first Sunday narrates the encounter between Christ and Satan whom he overcame by the power of God's word. The gospel of the second Sunday presents him in glory as he was being transfigured on the mountain, yet at that moment the cross that was the topic of his conversation with Moses and Elijah was already casting its long shadow upon his splendor and glory.

The Lenten Eucharist is our preparation for the feast of Easter. The daily liturgy moves onward to the culminating activity of the Easter Triduum, when the fullness of the paschal mystery is unfolded. In this sense, we may say that the Eucharist during the season of Lent prepares and celebrates the feast of Easter.

The Prayer over the Offerings exhorts us that as we commence in Lent the celebration of the paschal mystery of Christ we should shape our lives upon the holiness of the eucharistic bread and wine we offer.

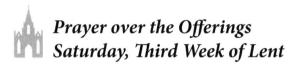

Prayer over the Offerings
Saturday, Third Week of Lent

O God, by whose grace it comes to pass
that we may approach your mysteries
with minds made pure,
grant, we pray,
that, in reverently handing them on,
we may offer you fitting homage.

> in reverently handing them on

Interpretation of the Text

The passage "in reverently handing them [mysteries] on" requires explaining. What are these mysteries and to whom do we hand them on? The Latin text says, "in eorum traditione sollemniter honoranda." What is the meaning of this somewhat obscure phrase? In the context of Prayers over the Offerings, *mysteria* is almost always the Eucharist itself; *traditio* (tradition) is a substantive and signifies the thing that has been handed on from the past. That tradition is the church's liturgical rite.[30] Hence, *traditio* stands for "institution." *Honorare*, on the other hand, is "the external manifestation, which is the festal celebration."[31] We may translate the oration literally as follows:

O God, by whose grace it comes
that we approach your mystery
with minds made pure,
grant, we pray,

that in solemnly celebrating its institution
we may offer fitting service.

In this prayer, tradition is not the act of handing on something to others; rather, it is the mystery, the sacred institution of the Eucharist, that has been handed on to us from the time of the apostles. The mystery, which we must approach with pure hearts, is the Eucharist.

> The sense of the Prayer over the Offerings is "In solemnly celebrating what has been handed on to us, which is the Eucharist, we offer you fitting service."

Homiletic-Catechetical Note

This prayer recalls 1 Corinthians 11:23: "For I received from the Lord what I also handed on to you, that the Lord Jesus, on the night he was handed over, took bread." The Eucharist, which we celebrate in obedience to the command of the Lord, is rooted in the tradition of the apostles. The Constitution on the Sacred Liturgy sublimely expresses this doctrine: "At the last supper, on the night he was betrayed, our Savior instituted the eucharistic sacrifice of his body and blood. This he did in order to perpetuate the sacrifice of the cross throughout the ages until he should come again" (47).

The celebration of the Eucharist binds the church to the apostolic tradition of the breaking of bread. It is the strongest assurance that the church comes from the apostles and will continue to exist until the return of the Lord at the end of the ages. The celebration of the Eucharist is the tradition that conveys to us across time and space the Last Supper, Calvary, and the resurrection of Christ. It is this tradition that unites us with the countless generations of the "saints" of God that celebrated and continue to celebrate the breaking of bread from the time of the apostles down to our own day.

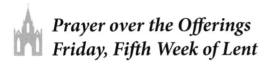

Prayer over the Offerings
Friday, Fifth Week of Lent

Grant, O merciful God, that we may be worthy
to serve ever fittingly at your altars,
and there to be saved by constant participation.

> to serve . . . at your altars

Interpretation of the Text

In the context of the eucharistic celebration, what are the "altars" referred to in this prayer? Where and how many are they? The Latin text is "digne tuis servire semper altaribus mereamur." "Altars" translates the plural *altaria*. Classical Latin and early liturgical usage employed *altaria*, the plural form of *altare*, to denote the altar of sacrifice. Latinists agree that the plural form of certain nouns from this period, such as *altare* and *sacrificium*, generally stands for the singular.

To make the message of the English oration easier to understand, we note the following observations. The plural noun "altars," which can occasion perplexity regarding the number of altars in the sanctuary, simply means altar. Christian theology affirms that there is only one altar of sacrifice, because there is only one sacrifice. Moreover, liturgical norms desire that sacred celebrations should be carried out at the same altar.[32] Lastly, the verb "to serve" carries the nuance of cultic celebration that is implied in the Latin *servire*.

> The sense of the Prayer over the Offerings is "May we be found worthy to celebrate Christ's sacrifice at the altar and be saved by continual participation in it."

Homiletic-Catechetical Note

"The altar, on which is effected the Sacrifice of the Cross made present under sacramental signs, is also the table of the Lord to which the People of God is convoked to participate in the Mass, and it is also the center of the thanksgiving that is accomplished through the Eucharist."[33]

The altar attains its full meaning in the sacrifice that is offered there through the ministry of the priest. Altar, sacrifice, and priesthood comprise the eucharistic offering of the church. The altar symbolizes Calvary, the cross, and the priesthood of Christ. We pray that we will be worthy to celebrate at this altar the sacrifice of Christ. What we see in the sanctuary is not just an altar; it is an altar of sacrifice.

But the altar also symbolizes the Last Supper table, where Jesus took the bread, broke it, and shared it with his disciples. Thus, the altar is likewise the table of the Lord. We celebrate his sacrifice and we partake of his Supper: this is what the Prayer over the Offerings tells us. The bread is broken in sacrifice, but it is shared as a meal. The altar is both Cenacle and Calvary.

The Sacred Paschal Triduum

Alternative Prayer
Good Friday

O God, who by the Passion of Christ your Son, our Lord,
abolished the death inherited from ancient sin
by every succeeding generation,
grant that just as, being conformed to him,
we have borne by the law of nature
the image of the man of earth,
so by the sanctification of grace
we may bear the image of the Man of heaven.

> 1. abolished the death inherited from ancient sin
> 2. just as, being conformed to him, / we have
>   borne by the law of nature / the image of the
>   man of earth

Interpretation of the Text

The phrase "the death inherited from ancient sin" is nuanced in the
Latin text. Sin was the cause of death. In this prayer, death is understood
primarily in the realm of the spiritual order: it is the loss of the life of
grace. The sense of the Latin text "peccati veteris hereditariam mortem"
is easy enough to grasp, but not as easy to translate literally. What it means
is, we inherited the death caused by sin.

It would be good if the position of the clause "being conformed to
him" accorded with the sentence structure of the Latin oration. As it is,
the passage is somewhat difficult to explain. Obviously the prayer is not
affirming that we bear the law of nature because we have been conformed

to Christ. The contrary is true: by being conformed to us, he bore the exigencies of nature. Restructured in agreement with the Latin text, the English translation reads as follows: "Grant that just as we have borne by law of nature the image of the man of earth, so by the sanctification of grace we, being conformed to him, may bear the image of the Man of heaven."

In this prayer "man of earth" seemingly refers to Adam, although it might be of interest to know that the Latin has *hominis*, which is an inclusive noun to mean female and male persons. On the other hand, "Man of heaven" is Christ himself. This expression, however, is quite peculiar. Below is a literal translation of the prayer:

> O God, who by the passion of Christ your Son, our Lord,
> brought to end primordial sin's inherited death
> to which every succeeding generation was subjected,
> grant that, just as we have borne by the law of nature
> the image of the earthly man,
> so, having been made in his likeness,
> we may bear by the sanctification of grace
> the image of the heavenly.

> The sense of this prayer is "We were created as earthly human beings, but by God's grace we were refashioned in the heavenly image of Christ."

Homiletic-Catechetical Note

The prayer that opens the Good Friday liturgy transports us to the primeval story of creation. The first sin of disobedience is recalled. Death entered into Paradise because of sin. More than merely causing physical death, it created the abysmal separation between God and the sinful human race. But the cross of Christ bridged the gap.

We can call this day Good Friday, because it was on this day when Jesus proved his goodness by shedding his blood for us. This day is also called Good Friday because it coincides with the sixth day of creation, which was the first Friday in the history of the universe. On that day God created our first parents. Gazing on his magnificent work, God declared that it was indeed very good.

But not everything that happened on this day was good. Early tradition tells us that it was also on Friday when the wily serpent tempted our first parents to eat the forbidden fruit. Deceived, they disobeyed God, lost God's friendship, and were driven out of Paradise.

We bind these traditions together in order to appreciate what we celebrate in the liturgy of Good Friday. It was on Friday when God created us; it was on Friday when sin was committed against God; and it was on Friday when God forgave our sins through the passion and death of the Son. From the opening prayer of Good Friday we can infer that God who is our Creator is also our Savior.

The story of Good Friday is echoed in our day in the lives of many people. Countless numbers of people suffer excruciating death brought about by sickness and violence. For them every single day is a Good Friday, because they suffer daily the squalor of poverty or are denied their basic human rights and dignity. They bear the image of earthly death: the prayer puts the hope in their hearts that the gloom of Good Friday will eventually give way to the joy of Easter and to their re-creation in the heavenly image of the risen Christ.

Prayer after the First Reading
The Easter Vigil

Almighty ever-living God,
who are wonderful in the ordering of all your works,
may those you have redeemed understand
that there exists nothing more marvelous
than the world's creation in the beginning
except that, at the end of the ages,
Christ our Passover has been sacrificed.

> there exists nothing more marvelous / than the
> world's creation in the beginning / except that, at
> the end of the ages, / Christ our Passover has
> been sacrificed

Interpretation of the Text

The sense of the English translation is not immediately clear, probably because of its clumsy construction: "nothing more marvelous / than . . . except that." The Latin text uses a verbal comparative clause: "non fuisse excellentius quod factus est mundus, quam quod Christus immolatus est." Its literal translation is this: "the fact that the world was created is not more exceptional than the fact that Christ was immolated"; but it is quite unwieldy and unsuitable for prayer. If we convert the verbs to nouns, the meaning will be easier to grasp and less awkward: "The creation of the world is not more admirable than the sacrifice of Christ." The following is a literal translation of this oration:

Almighty ever-living God,
who are wonderful in the dispensation of all your works,
let your redeemed people understand
that the creation of the world in the beginning
was not more wonderful
than the immolation of Christ our Passover
at the end of the ages.

> The sense of this prayer is "May God's redeemed people understand that the sacrifice of Christ our Passover at the end of the ages was more marvelous than the creation of the world in the beginning of time."

Homiletic-Catechetical Note

"Our birth would have been no gain, / had we not been redeemed." These words of the *Exsultet* echo the basic themes that lie beneath the marvelous works of God: creation and salvation. The vastness and order of the universe are breathtaking, but the prayer declares that the outcome and breadth of Christ's sacrifice far exceeds the marvels of creation. Christ's paschal mystery crowns God's work of creation. A new human race is formed from the ashes of sin to the image and likeness of the Savior.

This night's reading from the book of Genesis does not end on the Sabbath when God rested from all his works. It continues on in the celebration of Good Friday and Easter Vigil when a new human race is born from the side of Christ and nourished with the bread of life.

We recall that the Collect at the Mass during Christmas Day looks forward to the marvelous mystery of the Easter Vigil: "O God, who wonderfully created the dignity of human nature / and still more wonderfully restored it, / grant, we pray, / that we may share in the divinity of Christ, / who humbled himself to share in our humanity."

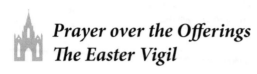

Prayer over the Offerings
The Easter Vigil

Accept, we ask, O Lord,
the prayers of your people
with the sacrificial offerings,
that what has begun in the paschal mysteries
may, by the working of your power,
bring us to the healing of eternity.

> 1. what has begun in the paschal mysteries
> 2. bring us to the healing of eternity

Interpretation of the Text

How do we interpret the clause "what has begun in the paschal mysteries"? The Latin is not simple to translate: *paschalibus initiata mysteriis*. *Initiata* is a plural noun, meaning the things that have been started. In Latin grammar, *paschalibus mysteriis* is a dative of reference. In this prayer the sense of the clause is "what we have begun with reference to the paschal mystery" or "what we have celebrated of the paschal mystery that is still in progress."[34] It is not a question of what has begun in the paschal mysteries. The phrase refers to the paschal mystery itself, which we have begun to celebrate in this Easter Vigil liturgy.

"Healing of eternity" is the new English translation of *aeternitatis medelam*. *Medela* usually means medicine or healing. In the Latin orations, the Eucharist is called *medela*. It restores the immortality that the human race had lost because of sin.[35] *Aeternitas*, on the other hand, often signifies immortality or eternal life. To explain this difficult Latin phrase, it helps to make the connection between the Eucharist, the paschal mystery, and the pledge of eternal life. *Aeternitatis medela* is the Eucharist; it restores immortality. The prayer may be translated literally as follows:

> Receive, we pray, O Lord,
> the prayers of your people with the offering of sacrifice,
> that the paschal mystery we have begun to celebrate
> may, by your working, restore immortality to us.

> The sense of this Prayer over the Offerings is "By his paschal mystery Christ regained for us eternal life. This is what we celebrate at Easter Vigil. The Eucharist we offer and receive is the pledge of immortality."

Homiletic-Catechetical Note

At Easter Vigil the celebration of the paschal mystery has just begun. It will go on in the course of the liturgical year in a cycle that starts with Advent. For the paschal mystery is the recurring theme of every liturgical season and feast. This is the message that underlies the oration's *paschalibus initiata mysteriis*. What we celebrate at Easter Vigil does not end there. Every time a person is baptized, it is Easter; every time man and woman are joined in the sacrament of marriage, it is Easter; every time sins are forgiven in the sacrament of penance, it is Easter; and, most of all, every time the Eucharist is offered, it is the Easter of the Lord's Supper, the Easter of his passion, death, and resurrection, and the Easter of the descent of the Holy Spirit.

The celebration of the paschal mystery will continue on even after the curtain shall have been rung down on the stage of history. Ancient Christian writers spoke about *triton pascha*, the three phases of Passover. The first was held by the Israelites, prefiguring the passage of Christ from this world to the Father. The second is Christ's own Passover, which prefigured our own when we passed from sin to new life across the waters of baptism. But there is another Passover, which is not of this world: it is the eternal banquet of the risen Lord, the banquet of immortality in the courts of heaven.

Easter Time

Collect
Tuesday within the Octave of Easter

O God, who have bestowed on us paschal remedies,
endow your people with heavenly gifts,
so that, possessed of perfect freedom,
they may rejoice in heaven
over what gladdens them now on earth.

paschal remedies

Interpretation of the Text

"Paschal remedies" translates *paschalia remedia*. But what does *remedia* mean? This word is found in several orations in Lent and Easter.[36] The word, both in singular and plural forms, is almost always associated with medicine and connotes an antidote.[37] To appreciate its use in liturgical texts, it is helpful to view it from the Christian perspective of human nature that was impaired by sin and is in need of God's healing.

In most instances, the orations speak of remedies in connection with the Eucharist, which has been called by the theologically significant name "antidote of the resurrection."[38] What it means is that the risen Body of Christ in the Eucharist is an antidote for sin and hence is pledge of future resurrection. "Perfect freedom," on the other hand, is freedom from sin; it is the freedom granted to us by Christ's eucharistic Body, which is the paschal remedy for our sins. Hence, in this oration, "remedies" refers to the glorious Body of Christ in the Eucharist. It is called "paschal remedies" because their healing power flows forth from Christ's death and resurrection.

The sense of "remedies" in these and other orations is "In the Eucharist God gives us Christ's glorified Body, which is remedy for the spiritual illness of our fallen nature and a pledge of our resurrection on the last day."

Homiletic-Catechetical Note

The Collect calls to mind Christ's discourse on the bread of life: "Whoever eats my flesh and drinks my blood has eternal life, and I will raise him on the last day" (John 6:54). Eucharistic Communion refers to spiritual nourishment as well as to cleansing from sins and protection from them. The Eucharist is both food and remedy.

Saint Ambrose has a beautiful and inspiring catechetical discourse about the healing quality of the Eucharist: "If, as often as his blood is shed, it is shed for the forgiveness of sins, I should always receive it, so that it may always forgive my sins. Because I always sin, I should always have a remedy."[39]

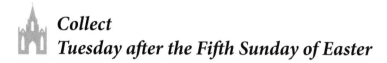

Collect
Tuesday after the Fifth Sunday of Easter

O God, who restore us to eternal life
in the Resurrection of Christ,
grant your people constancy in faith and hope,
that we may never doubt the promises
of which we have learned from you.

> 1. constancy in faith and hope
> 2. the promises / of which we have learned from you

Interpretation of the Text

There is a shade of distinction between "constancy in faith and hope" and "the constancy of faith and hope." The Latin text puts across the latter: it defines the nature of the theological virtues of faith and hope more than the quality of our constancy in them. Such nuance is not insignificant. We do not doubt God's promises, because we cling to the firmness of faith and hope, not to our own determination to be steadfast in these virtues.

The passage "the promises / of which we have learned from you" can be reexpressed, for easier comprehension, to read, "The promises that you as their author have made." The key phrase here is the Latin ablative absolute *te auctore*: "Having you as the author or originator" or, in other words, "On your own initiative." It points to God's initiative and our confidence that if the promises were made by God, we will not be disappointed. The following is a literal translation of this Collect:

O God, who in the resurrection of Christ
restore us for eternal life,
give to your people the constancy of faith and hope,
that we may not doubt that the promises,
which we know you made on your own initiative,
will be fulfilled.

> The sense of the Collect is "On the firm foundation
> of faith and hope we do not doubt that what God
> promised will be fulfilled in our lives."

Homiletic-Catechetical Note

The Collect recalls to mind the Canticles of Zechariah and the Blessed
Mother: "He promised . . . to show mercy to our fathers [ancestors]"
and "He has . . . remember[ed] his mercy, / according to his promise to
our fathers" (Luke 1:70, 72, 54-55). We ask God to establish us upon the
rock of faith and hope, so that we will not doubt God's promises. What
are those promises? What is the oath that he swore to our ancestors? The
Collect answers by pointing to the promised possession of eternal life,
which the resurrection of Christ has gained for us.

God is faithful and will fulfill what God has promised. The Collect
goes a step farther by invoking divine initiative. We did not have the
capacity to ask; God promised of God's own accord: *te auctore*. Everything
is God's free gift. We have always known this. Our adoption as children,
our share in the eucharistic banquet, and countless other divine blessings:
we have received all this from the overflowing generosity of God's love.
We did not ask; God gave. And when we dared to ask, it was because God
had planted faith and hope in our hearts. This we have always known and
we have never been disappointed.

Collect
Vigil Mass of Pentecost

> Almighty ever-living God,
> who willed the Paschal Mystery
> to be encompassed as a sign in fifty days,
> grant that from out of the scattered nations
> the confusion of many tongues
> may be gathered by heavenly grace
> into one great confession of your name.

> 1. to be encompassed as a sign in fifty days
> 2. the confusion of many tongues / may be gathered . . . into one

Interpretation of the Text

For a fuller appreciation of this Collect, we need to examine the meaning of several words and phrases. How do we interpret "sign," "fifty days," "from out of the scattered nations," and "confusion of many tongues"? What is the meaning of the petition "grant that . . . the confusion of many tongues / may be gathered . . . into one great confession"? Below is a literal translation of the Latin text as aid to textual analysis of the Collect:

> Almighty ever-living God,
> who willed that the paschal sacrament
> should be encompassed by the mystery of fifty days,
> grant that the differences of languages

brought about by the dispersion of nations
may be gathered together by heavenly grace
for a single confession of your name.

To grasp the message of the English version of this Collect, we make recourse to the Latin text. For "sign" the Latin has *mysterio* and for "fifty days," *quinquaginta dierum*, or "the mystery of fifty days." Since Pentecost means fifty days, the phrase means "the mystery of Pentecost." Hence, the passage means that the paschal mystery is encompassed by the fifty days culminating in the mystery of Pentecost. On this day the oration speaks of two mysteries: the paschal sacrament (mystery) and the mystery of Pentecost.

"From out of the scattered nations" refers to the Latin ablative absolute *gentium facta dispersione*. It is a statement of fact that nations have been dispersed and that dispersion has given rise to the diversity of languages.

"Confusion of many tongues" is a free translation of *divisiones linguarum*. *Divisio* means diversity or differences; it does not necessarily involve or entail confusion. "Confusion" might have been suggested by the story of the tower of Babel, but the Collect is more pertinently inspired by the account in the Acts of the Apostles (2:8) on the day of Pentecost: "Then how does each of us hear them in his own native language?" Hence, confusion stands here for diversity. What we ask from God at Pentecost is unity in diversity. We profess the same belief in different languages.

> The sense of the Collect is "God wanted that the paschal mystery should be encompassed by the mystery of Pentecost. May he bring together for the confession of his name the diverse languages that arose from the dispersal of the nations."

Homiletic-Catechetical Note

Christ died, rose again, and ascended into heaven in order to send the Holy Spirit. The first part of the Collect intimates that the mystery of Pentecost was the culmination of the paschal mystery. Pentecost Sunday signaled that the era of the Holy Spirit in the church had begun. From that time on, the Holy Spirit has been enlightening the church about the words and actions of Christ, guiding the course of its history, protecting it from harm, and bringing out new things from the treasury of its tradition.

In the liturgy we recall through rites and prayers the entire mystery of the risen Lord. This action is what liturgists call *anamnesis*. In order that we will experience the presence and effect of the mystery, the church invokes the intervention of the Holy Spirit. Liturgists call this *epiclesis*. Every liturgical celebration, in as much as it is the *anamnesis* of the paschal mystery, is also the bestowal of the Holy Spirit.

Moreover, the Collect, by alluding to the event of Pentecost Sunday, calls attention to the missionary character of the church. All nations must hear the message of the risen Christ in their own language; the message must be woven into their cultural fabric; every people must be given the opportunity to worship God according to what is noble, true, and beautiful in their culture and traditions.

Ordinary Time

Prayer over the Offerings
Second Sunday in Ordinary Time

Grant us, O Lord, we pray,
that we may participate worthily in these mysteries,
for whenever the memorial of this sacrifice is celebrated
the work of our redemption is accomplished.

> the work of our redemption is accomplished

Interpretation of the Text

The Latin text reads, "opus nostrae redemptionis exercetur." The verb *exercere* is not the same as *perficere* or *exsequi*. The former means "carrying out" an action without implying its completion. The latter, on the other hand, supposes the successful conclusion of the work; this is the usual meaning we attach to the verb "accomplish."

When we explain the sense of this oration, we should keep in mind that in the liturgy the work of our redemption is not as yet brought to a close. Christ accomplished it, perfected it upon the cross, but each one of us must still welcome it and experience its saving effect in our lives. This is what *exercetur* means. The following is a literal translation of the oration:

Grant us, we pray, O Lord,
to take part worthily in this sacrament,
for, as often as the memorial of this sacrifice is celebrated,
the work of our redemption is performed.

79

> The sense of the oration is "In the celebration of the
> liturgy in which the sacrifice of Christ is made
> present, the work of our redemption continues to
> be carried out."

Homiletic-Catechetical Note

The Constitution on the Sacred Liturgy teaches that "the liturgy, then, is rightly seen as an exercise of the priestly office of Jesus Christ" (7). This conciliar doctrine reaffirms the Prayer over the Offerings. In the liturgy Christ is at hand to exercise his priestly office through the rites and prayers of the church, so that the sacrifice on the altar of Calvary may be perpetuated throughout the ages on the table of the Eucharist.

In the Prayer over the Offerings we beg God to make us worthy to participate in the mystery. It is by participating that we take hold of the grace of redemption. From this belief the conciliar Constitution draws the fundamental principle of the liturgical reform of Vatican II: active and conscious participation. This is the bedrock of the Constitution on the Sacred Liturgy. It is also the spirit that permeates the entire project of the conciliar liturgical reform. In the minds of the council fathers the most effective way for the faithful to avail themselves of the spiritual benefits of the liturgy is through full and active participation.

To guarantee active participation the Constitution directs that "both texts and rites should be ordered so as to express more clearly the holy things which they signify. The christian people, as far as is possible, should be able to understand them easily and take part in them in a celebration which is full, active and the community's own" (21). Clarity of the rites and texts and understanding them with ease are the hallmarks of the reform.

To promote active participation, the council fathers approved the use of the vernacular, the revision of the Tridentine rites, the creation of new rites if opportune, greater involvement of the laity in liturgical ministries, and the adaptation of the liturgy to the culture and traditions of peoples. Ultimately the aim of all these programs of reform is worthy participation in the celebration of Christ's mystery.

Collect
Fourth Sunday in Ordinary Time

Grant us, Lord our God,
that we may honor you with all our mind,
and love everyone in truth of heart.

---

1. honor you with all our mind
2. love everyone in truth of heart

Interpretation of the Text

The Latin original of this Collect dates from the sixth century.[40] Its message echoes the greatest commandment: "You shall love the Lord, your God, with all your heart, with all your soul, and with all your mind. . . . You shall love your neighbor as yourself" (Matt 22:37, 39). Thus, the petition is twofold: to honor God and to love everyone.

The Latin employs here the verb *venerare* whose equivalent in the English Collect is "honor." This is the only instance in the Latin Missal when this verb is used in reference to God. The choice of *venerare* instead of the more common *adorare* sends an important message. The notion of *venerare*, unlike *adorare*, includes cultic, external rite or, in short, liturgical worship. We adore God with all our mind, but we express our worship externally by means of liturgical celebration. "With all our mind" (*tota mente*) alludes to the commandment; it implies heart and soul or the entire person.

The second petition is a prayer that we will love everyone "in truth of heart" or, in other words, with a sincere heart. The Latin is *rationabili affectu*, whose literal translation is "spiritual affection."[41] *Affectus* is feeling or disposition of the heart. It is the affection one feels for another person; it involves human sentiments and emotions, not the intellect alone. *Rationabilis*, on the other hand, connotes more than true or sincere love. It represents what is noblest in a person, namely, the spirit, the highest level of human consciousness. Christian affection goes beyond what is carnal and psychological: it dwells in the realm of the spirit. Here is a possible translation, which is not literal, though warranted by biblical teaching:

> Grant us, Lord our God,
> that we may worship you with our whole heart
> and love everyone with spiritual affection.

> The sense of the Collect is "Through acts of worship may we honor God with all our heart and may we love everyone with spiritual affection."

Homiletic-Catechetical Note

Volumes have been written about the greatest commandment. Is there any new insight we can gain from this Collect? The Latin text pairs *venerare mente* with *diligere affectu*. We worship God with our mind and love our neighbor with our heart. However, we worship God not only with our mind but also by means of external rites: this is what the Collect wishes to impress on us when it uses the verb *venerare*.

Yet, participation in liturgical worship does not remain on the level of ceremonies. It is an activity of mind, soul, and heart. The commandment is to love God, but love of God comprises worship. Through acts that are perceptible to the senses we love and adore God whom we cannot see. In the liturgy God is as large as life; through the sacred rites we behold and touch God's face.

The second part of the commandment is love of neighbor. Unlike God, our neighbor is made of flesh and bones, but love must transcend the physical, or, better yet, love must spring from *rationabili affectu*.

Prayer over the Offerings
Fifth Sunday in Ordinary Time

O Lord our God,
who once established these created things
to sustain us in our frailty,
grant, we pray,
that they may become for us now
the Sacrament of eternal life.

who once established these created things

Interpretation of the Text

In the context of this Prayer over the Offerings, "these created things" obviously mean the elements of bread and wine on the altar. It might sound quite odd to refer to them as "these created things," but there is a particular reason for this. It reminds us that God is the Creator of bread and wine, the food and drink that nourish us both bodily and spiritually. The theme is repeated like a refrain in several other Prayers over the Offerings.

The expression "established these created things" is awkward, but any attempt to translate *condidisti* literally would result in a redundant sentence: "God created these created things." A freer translation of *condidisti* elucidates the meaning of the English text: "God provides us with bread and wine for our bodily sustenance."

The English oration contrasts "once" and "now": once God created them for our bodily nourishment; now God transforms them into the sacrament of eternal life. The Latin text, on the other hand, uses the adverbs *potius* and *etiam* to say that these elements serve a double purpose. Thus, the English version should not be interpreted to mean that in the past God created them for one purpose and now God uses them for another. The following is a literal translation of the oration:

> Lord our God,
> who provide us with these created things
> for the sustenance of our frailty,
> grant, we pray,
> that they may also become for us
> the sacrament of immortality.

> The sense of the oration is "The Creator continues to provide the bread and wine we need. When they are placed on our tables, they are food and drink for our corporal sustenance; when they are placed on the altar, they become the sacrament of eternal life."

Homiletic-Catechetical Note

The prayer of blessing over the bread and wine at the offertory rite resonates with this ancient Prayer over the Offerings. "Blessed are you, Lord God of all creation, / for through your goodness we have received / the bread (wine) we offer you: / fruit of the earth (fruit of the vine) and work of human hands, / it will become for us the bread of life (it will become our spiritual drink)."

Bread and wine: these are fruits of the earth and the products of human labor. At Holy Mass they will become for us the sacraments of Christ's Body and Blood. To become human, he needed the cooperation of a woman. To become the sacrament of the Eucharist, he needs the collaboration of Mother Earth and the industry of laborers. It is amazing to think that the Creator of the universe is, of his own volition, dependent on the fields of wheat and the vineyards and the work of human hands.

But the Eucharist is something larger than bread and wine. These are symbols of God's boundless concern for the well-being of humankind. They urge us to take a hard look at the world around us. People are hungry. Beggars roam our streets, knocking on the windows of cars pleading for alms, offering services for a pittance. Mother Earth's resources are despoiled by human greed. Farms that once produced sufficient food have been converted to high-earning subdivisions and golf courses. Yet many of the urban poor are homeless. In the name of development trees are mercilessly cut down and mountains are unscrupulously leveled or mined. The bread and wine we offer rally us to fight unbridled economic development at the expense of local people and natural environment.

Prayer after Communion
Ninth Sunday in Ordinary Time

Govern by your Spirit, we pray, O Lord,
those you feed with the Body and Blood of your Son,
that, professing you not just in word or in speech,
but also in works and in truth,
we may merit to enter the Kingdom of Heaven.

> Govern . . . those you feed . . . [that] we
> may merit

Interpretation of the Text

The shift from the third to the first person ("those you feed" and "we may merit") might cause minor confusion. The oration does not deal with two groups of people: them and us. At first reading, the passage might be wrongly interpreted: "Govern them, so that we may merit to enter heaven." The Latin text says, "rege nos quos pascis." The following is a literal translation of the oration:

O Lord, by your Spirit govern us, we pray,
whom you feed with the Body and Blood of your Son,
that, professing you not just in word or in speech,
but also in works and in truth,
we may merit to enter the Kingdom of Heaven.

> The sense of the oration is "Lord, by your Spirit
> govern us whom you feed with the Body and Blood
> of Christ, so that we may merit to enter heaven."

Homiletic-Catechetical Note

Several themes are at work in this short oration. On the whole, they direct our thoughts to Psalm 23, the psalm of the good shepherd. Its first line of this psalm in Latin is "Dominus regit me: nihil mihi deerit." Its literal translation is "The Lord rules me: I shall not want anything." The English translation of this oration ("Govern . . . those you feed") may thus be read in the light of Psalm 23. God is our shepherd: God governs and feeds us.

God shepherds his people by leading them to the pasture of Christ's Body and Blood. The verb *regere* connotes divine providence,[42] which is characterized in this prayer by feeding (*pascere*). God as shepherd not only rules but also provides. God rules the people by the wisdom of the Spirit and provides them with the spiritual nourishment of the Eucharist.

The second portion of the oration is an allusion to the parable of the lost lamb. Against any such possibility or eventuality we pray that we may not depart from the watchful care of our Shepherd and thus enter at last the kingdom of heaven.

Christ is the shepherd and he calls us his lambs. We know that lambs are somewhat helpless and dull compared to goats. But because he is always on the side of the disparaged, in his parable of the Last Judgment he favors the lambs over the goats. He surely cares for the goats as well. But goats can fend for themselves. They have a higher rating for survival than lambs. Lambs may be innocent and harmless, but they are dreary creatures that cannot help themselves out of the pit. They venture out of the fold but cannot retrace their way back. They are led to be slaughtered but cannot find voice to protest. These are unflattering traits, but we find comfort in the thought that because we are weak, Christ rules our lives, feeds us with his Body and Blood, and leads us to the eternal sheepfold.

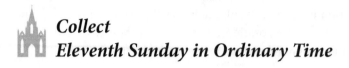

Collect
Eleventh Sunday in Ordinary Time

O God, strength of those who hope in you,
graciously hear our pleas,
and, since without you mortal frailty can do nothing,
grant us always the help of your grace,
that in following your commands
we may please you by our resolve and our deeds.

> without you mortal frailty can do nothing

Interpretation of the Text

This Collect comes from the seventh-century Gelasian Sacramentary.[43] It belongs to the classic collection of Latin orations whose *cursus*, balance, and inverted word order yield a sonorous rhythm. Except for the phrase *mortalis infirmitas*, the Latin Collect is not difficult to understand.

"Mortal frailty" is a literal translation of *mortalis infirmitas*. What does the phrase mean? In some Latin orations *mortalis* is substituted with *humana*: human frailty. It is redundant to say that frailty is mortal. Moreover, "frailty" as subject makes the sentence somewhat abstract and consequently distances itself from the immediate experience of the listeners.[44] However, this difficulty is of minor significance as far as understanding the text is concerned.

A possible way to translate the phrase is to regard the adjective *mortalis* as substantive and the substantive *infirmitas* as adjective: *infirmi mortales* (frail mortal beings).[45] In Latin, such interchange of the grammatical function of substantives and adjectives is not unheard of. Below is a literal translation of the Collect:

God, strength of those who hope in you,
mercifully draw near to our prayers,
and since without you frail mortals can do nothing,
grant always the help of your grace,
that in keeping your commands,
we may please you in will and in action.

> The sense of the Collect is "Since frail mortals that
> we are can do nothing without you, grant us always
> the help of your grace."

Homiletic-Catechetical Note

The Collect brings to mind Christ's declaration: "without me you can do nothing" (John 15:5). "Mortal frailty" refers primarily to our inability to attain heaven without the help of God. On our own, we falter in our relationship with God whose grace must precede, accompany, and follow all our thoughts and actions, if they are to please God.

However, the Collect and Christ's warning should not be confined to the realm of spiritual life. Human race continues to progress with giant strides in science and technology, often unaware of the creative hand of God behind every successful human endeavor. Sometimes scientific discoveries are exploited to contest Christ's universal dominion. But according to our belief as Christians, he gained ascendancy over the entire creation through his paschal mystery.

The entire creation encompasses whatever the human race has achieved. Everything came from God to whom we must bow in recognition of God's sovereignty.

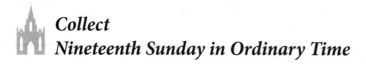

Collect
Nineteenth Sunday in Ordinary Time

Almighty ever-living God,
whom, taught by the Holy Spirit,
we dare to call our Father,
bring, we pray, to perfection in our hearts
the spirit of adoption as your sons and daughters,
that we may merit to enter into the inheritance
which you have promised.

> God, / whom, taught by the Holy Spirit, / we dare
> to call our Father

Interpretation of the Text

This Collect "shows the genius of the Roman rite, its noble simplicity, and its integration of majesty and intimacy, as seen in the majestic invocation, and its intimate amplification and in the petition."[46] The invocation is stately: *Omnipotens sempiterne Deus*; on the other hand, the amplification and petition are more personal: *paterno nomine* and *adoptionis filiorum*.

One minor observation on the English translation of this text concerns the word order: "God, / whom, taught by the Holy Spirit, / we dare to call our Father." It is obvious that the clause "taught by the Holy Spirit" is linked to "we," not to "whom." No one would ever think that God is taught by the Holy Spirit. Nonetheless, the construction of this sentence can be improved by putting the clause "taught by the Holy Spirit" in its proper place. The Latin uses here the ablative absolute *docente Spiritu Sancto*, which can be rendered by an adverbial clause: "God, whom, as the Holy Spirit teaches, we dare to call our Father." We may translate the Latin Collect literally as follows:

> Almighty ever-living God,
> whom we, by the teaching of the Holy Spirit
> dare to call with the name of Father,
> bring, we pray, to perfection in our hearts
> the spirit of the adoption of children,
> that we may merit to enter
> into the promised inheritance.

> The sense of the Collect is "Taught by the Holy Spirit, we dare to call God our Father."

Homiletic-Catechetical Note

The Collect is an impressive, perfect blending of the two attitudes we should have when we enter into the presence of God: reverential awe and childlike confidence. In this prayer we address God as "Almighty ever-living God." In fact, in the entire corpus of orations in the Roman Missal God is rarely called Father. The invocation "Almighty God" is definitely influenced by the notion of the liturgy as worship of divine majesty. In the liturgy we do not appear before God in a nonchalant, casual manner.

Profound respect, however, is not a synonym of distance and detachment. When we pray to almighty ever-living God, we do not address someone who is totally beyond our reach, who lives in an unapproachable light, who is not concerned with the affairs of the human race. Christ's incarnation has bridged the eternal gap between the divine and the human. He taught us to call God our Father (Luke 11:1). The Collect reminds us that we have received the spirit of adoption as sons and daughters of the Father.

Thus, while we bow our heads or prostrate ourselves before God's presence, our hearts speak with childlike confidence to a Father, the Father of our Lord Jesus Christ.

Prayer after Communion
Twenty-Fifth Sunday in Ordinary Time

Graciously raise up, O Lord,
those you renew with this Sacrament,
that we may come to possess your redemption
both in mystery and in the manner of our life.

> both in mystery and in the manner of our life

Interpretation of the Text

The English version of this prayer does not translate *continuis auxiliis* (continued help) and *effectum* (effect). Although the latter may be considered implied, the former is an important theological component of prayer and should not be taken for granted. We are in need of God's continued pouring of grace.

The new translation takes *sacramentis* to mean the sacrament, that is, Holy Communion. This interpretation is in consonance with the context of the prayer.

But what does "in mystery" (*mysteriis*) mean in this oration? The Latin word *mysteriis* is in the ablative case. It is an ablative of means. A plausible interpretation of *mysteriis* in this particular instance is the liturgical rite itself. It is paired conveniently with *moribus*. The repetition of the conjunction *et* (both/and) strongly stresses the unity between worship and life. The following is a literal translation of this oration:

Gracious Lord, with continual help sustain us
whom you refresh with your sacrament,

that we may receive the effect of redemption
both by the mysteries and manner of life.

> The sense of the phrase is "By means of the myster-
> ies we celebrate and the manner of life we live may
> we receive the effect of redemption."

Homiletic-Catechetical Note

Worship and life, like faith and good works, express the Christian program of life. They are closely allied. Meaningful worship exerts great influence over the quality of our life and, vice-versa, the good life we live makes our worship an intense experience of God. *Mysteria* and *mores*, worship and life, *ora et labora*: they all convey in different words the message of the oration: not prayer alone, not work alone, but a harmonious balance of both.

This post-Communion prayer addresses itself to those who have received the Eucharist. Thus, the connection between worship and life is further defined in the context of Holy Communion. There is a kind of trilogy here: Holy Communion, liturgical participation, and manner of life. The prayer is that God will sustain by grace those whom God has nourished with the sacrament of Christ's Body and Blood, so that by prayer and work they may attain salvation.

 *Collect*
The Most Holy Trinity

God our Father, who by sending into the world
the Word of truth and the Spirit of sanctification
made known to the human race your wondrous mystery,
grant us, we pray, that in professing the true faith,
we may acknowledge the Trinity of eternal glory
and adore your Unity, powerful in majesty.

> 1. acknowledge the Trinity of eternal glory
> 2. adore your Unity

Interpretation of the Text

A number of things need to be clarified about this English Collect.[47] The wording of the petition could be theologically misleading, if it is not carefully explained. The following is a literal translation of the Latin Collect:

God the Father, who by sending into the world
the Word of truth and the Spirit of sanctification
revealed to the human race your wondrous mystery,
grant us, in the confession of the true faith,
to acknowledge the glory of the eternal Trinity
and to adore the Unity in the power of majesty.

It should be pointed out that the Latin text does not say "acknowledge the Trinity of eternal glory" but "acknowledge the glory of the eternal

Trinity." The object of the verb *agnoscere* (to acknowledge) is the glory of the Trinity, not the Trinity whom we adore, not merely acknowledge. The wording of the English oration should be explained with great care to steer clear of doctrinal inaccuracy.

Somewhat more disturbing from a theological standpoint is the second petition "and adore your Unity, powerful in majesty." How is the Latin text formulated? To begin with, it has no possessive pronoun (your). The insertion of "your" is what causes the problem in the English translation. The Latin text simply states "adore the Unity in the power of majesty."

It is useful to remember that the one addressed in this prayer is God the Father, not the holy Trinity. In the new English translation the phrase "your Unity" would seem to refer to the Father, unless by the application of some elliptical device we complete the statement so that it would read as follows: "Father, we adore your Unity with the Word of truth and the Spirit of sanctification." As the English version stands, we are given the wrong impression that we adore the Unity of God the Father. This is certainly not an insignificant theological issue. The passage is inaccurate and should be rectified by deleting the possessive pronoun "your." What the Latin text says is "We adore the Unity [of the three Divine Persons] in the power of majesty."

We are familiar with the expression "adore the Holy Trinity," not "adore the Holy Unity." When we explain the Collect of the Holy Trinity, it might help to remember what these statements mean. We adore the Godhead in a Trinity of Persons; we adore the same Godhead in the Unity of the three Persons: the Father, the Son, and the Holy Spirit.

It can be argued that the phrase "your Unity" means the mystery of the holy Trinity, which God the Father had kept hidden and finally revealed through Christ and the Holy Spirit. But that is not a convincing justification for adding "your" to the text.

> The sense of the Collect is "When we make the profession of faith, we acknowledge the glory of the Father, the Son, and the Holy Spirit whom we adore as three Persons united in one divine majesty."

Homiletic-Catechetical Note

We begin the celebration of the Mass making the sign of the cross while the priest recites, "In the name of the Father, and of the Son, and of the Holy Spirit." We combine the sign of the cross with the name of the holy Trinity to remind ourselves that we have been convened to celebrate the Eucharist in the name of the three Divine Persons. We do likewise for the other liturgical rites to assure us that the holy Trinity whom we invoke as we start the celebration is in our midst.

It was by the will and authority of the Father and with the energy of the Holy Spirit that Jesus, the Word of truth, preached the truth about the Father and took up the cross to Calvary. When he gave up his life with loud cries and tears of supplication, the ugliness of human sin was magnified, but the loving compassion of the holy Trinity was revealed and the Holy Spirit descended to sanctify those for whom Jesus had died.

The holy Trinity will always remain a mystery of our faith, but the incarnation and the paschal mystery of Christ together with the mystery of Pentecost have unveiled for us the eternal Trinity and Unity of the Godhead and made the three Persons as large as life.

Prayer after Communion
The Most Holy Trinity

May receiving this Sacrament, O Lord our God,
bring us health of body and soul,
as we confess your eternal holy Trinity and undivided Unity.

> we confess your eternal holy Trinity and
> undivided Unity

Interpretation of the Text

The opening line of the new English translation would flow better if the more common noun "reception" were used: "May the reception of this Sacrament bring us . . . " We take note of the verb *proficiat*, which is rendered here as "bring." *Proficere* has several meanings. "In its transferred sense, this verb occurs rather frequently to express the inner sacramental action of the Eucharist."[48] It is used in the sense of "to advance," "to draw profit from," "to be of advantage to," or, in this oration, "to promote." But these are matters of minor importance.

What is of major concern and causes perplexity in the new English translation is the phrase "your eternal holy Trinity and undivided Unity." Here, as in the preceding oration, God the Father is addressed. It is theologically misleading to speak about the holy Trinity and undivided Unity of God the Father. It is a lapse, certainly unconscious, and should be accurately explained and remedied by expunging "your" from the text.

Again it can be argued that "your Trinity and Unity" refers to the eternal mystery that the Father revealed through Christ and the Holy Spirit. However, the textual analysis of this prayer does not allow us to

97

entertain the insertion of the possessive pronoun "your." Below is a literal translation of this oration:

> Lord God,
> may the reception of this sacrament
> and the confession of the everlasting holy Trinity
> and the undivided Unity of the same
> promote the health of our body and soul.

> The sense of the oration is "Holy Communion and profession of faith in the Holy Trinity have their holistic effect upon the person of a believer."

Homiletic-Catechetical Note

Not infrequently we tend to segregate the things of the soul and spirit from the things that pertain to our body. What, for example, has Holy Communion, or, for that matter, our trinitarian profession of faith, to do with our physical, corporal reality?

This Prayer after Communion, however, offers a surprising insight on the holistic character of the human person. There is a continuous flow of influence from the spirit to the body and from the body to the spirit. Holy Communion is not an action of the soul alone, but of the human body as well.

Likewise the profession of faith, performed in the context of personal relationship with each Person of the holy Trinity, affects not only the intellect but the heart as well. It is good to remind ourselves that the manifestation of the holy Trinity was done in the reality of Christ's human body, soul, and spirit. We get a glimpse of the triune God by the words spoken by Christ, by his works of mercy and forgiveness, and by his bodily suffering. If we but listen attentively with our hearts, we can also sense the indwelling of the Spirit in the reality of our earthly being. Yes, as the Prayer after Communion wants us to realize, our profession of belief in the holy Trinity can have a profound effect upon the body and soul, mind and spirit, heart and intellect of the human person.

Prayer over the Offerings
Corpus Christi

Grant your Church, O Lord, we pray,
the gifts of unity and peace,
whose signs are to be seen in mystery
in the offerings we here present.

> whose signs are to be seen in mystery

Interpretation of the Text

In this oration what meaning do we give to the complex phrase "whose signs are to be seen in mystery"? As noted earlier in the general observations, depending on the context, the liturgical word "mysteries" or "mystery" can mean the doctrine of faith, the Eucharist, or the liturgical rite. But if we check the Latin text, what we find is *mystice*, not *in mysterio*. Hence, the offerings on the altar symbolize mystically, that is to say in a sacred and spiritual manner, God's gift of unity and peace.[49] The Latin oration's *mystice* makes no allusion to the liturgical mystery. It speaks about the way in which God's gifts of unity and peace are signified. The following is a literal translation of this oration:

Gracious Lord,
grant your Church, we pray,
the gift of unity and peace,
which are mystically signified
by the offerings we make.

99

> The sense of this Prayer over the Offerings is "The eucharistic offering of bread and wine laid on the altar is a mystical symbol of God's gift of unity and peace."

Homiletic-Catechetical Note

The bread and wine on the altar are destined to become the sacraments of Christ's Body and Blood. This is the theme that dominates the Prayers over the Offerings. Sometimes the orations anticipate what is yet to take place during the eucharistic prayer.

The prayer we are examining gives another dimension to the eucharistic elements we place on the altar. They symbolize in a mystical way Christ's gift of unity and peace. The liturgical rite we celebrate brings us back to the Last Supper when Christ promised to give us his peace and to Calvary where he offered his body and blood to gain for us unity and peace with God.

Proper of Saints

Collect
The Visitation of the Blessed Virgin Mary, May 31

Almighty ever-living God,
who, while the Blessed Virgin Mary was carrying your Son in
    her womb,
inspired her to visit Elizabeth,
grant us, we pray,
that, faithful to the promptings of the Spirit,
we may magnify your greatness
with the Virgin Mary at all times.

> that . . . we may magnify your greatness / with
> the Virgin Mary

Interpretation of the Text

The message of this English oration, though expressed lengthily, is
not difficult to grasp. But in contrast with the noble simplicity of classical
Roman orations, it is somewhat long-winded and consequently difficult
to proclaim in the liturgical assembly. The last two lines are somewhat
disappointing. "Magnify your greatness" is a redundant passage, and the
phrase "with the Virgin Mary at all times" dangles. Besides, the English
"magnify" is not a suitable equivalent of *magnificare*.[50] Moreover, the
sentence construction "magnify your greatness / with the Virgin Mary"
is ambiguous, although no one will probably take it to mean God's greatness with Mary. Below is a literal translation of this Collect:

Almighty ever-living God,
who inspired the Blessed Virgin Mary, while she bore your Son,
to visit Elizabeth,
grant, we pray, that obedient to the inspiring Spirit,
we, together with her, may be able to glorify you always.

> The sense of the Collect is "We pray that in imita-
> tion of the Virgin Mary we will listen to the Holy
> Spirit who inspires us to come to the assistance of
> people who are in need."

Homiletic-Catechetical Note

When Mary learned from the angel that her cousin Elizabeth had conceived in her old age, she hastened to visit her. Her cousin needed a younger woman to do the house chores. She was carrying the Son of God in her womb, but she was oblivious of her dignity. Someone needed her help; it was not the time to think of status and rank. She stayed with her cousin for three months until John was born. That was the kind of person Mary was, and that was the kind of humility and charity the Child in her womb was imbibing from his mother. At the sound of Mary's greeting of peace, the infant in Elizabeth's womb leaped for joy, as he "sensed the hidden presence of Christ" (Prayer after Communion).

The story of the visitation repeats itself daily on our altar. There, by the mysterious words proclaimed by the priest, Christ comes to visit his people. He hides himself under the cloak of sacrament, but our faith allows us to "sense" his presence in the elements of bread and wine. The visitation teaches us to recognize the church as the mother that brings forth the sacrament of Christ's Body and Blood.

We pray that God will grant us the grace to "sense" Christ's presence in every person who comes to assist us in our need. And when our turn comes, we imitate the humility and charity of Mary. Prompted by the Holy Spirit, we go an extra mile in order to come to the help of our brothers and sisters.

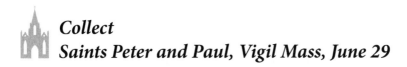

Collect
Saints Peter and Paul, Vigil Mass, June 29

Grant, we pray, O Lord our God,
that we may be sustained
by the intercession of the blessed Apostles Peter and Paul,
that, as through them you gave your Church
the foundations of her heavenly office,
so through them you may help her to eternal salvation.

> the foundations of her heavenly office

Interpretation of the Text

At first glance this English Collect does not seem to require a second look. But there is a passage in it that should be clarified. "Foundations of her heavenly office" is intended to translate *superni munus rudimenta*. The meaning of this Latin phrase is not as obvious and simple as the English rendering of it. The Latin *rudimenta* is the same as the English "rudiment." Both imply earliest stage of development, as in the expression *rudimenta fidei* (rudiments of faith). Foundation and rudiment are not synonyms. In fact, Latin uses *fundamentum* when foundation is intended.

In the Latin liturgy, *munus* is *crux interpretationis*. "A very prolific word in the Orations, it deserves careful investigation; for it displays quite a nuanced character."[51] Although nuances can be detected in the Prayers over the Offerings and Prayers after Communion, the basic meaning of *munus* is gift. Only once does it appear (in the Collect for a dead priest) with the meaning of priestly honor and duty (*sacris muneribus*).

"Foundations of her heavenly office" is a comforting thought; it is an assurance that God laid the foundations of the church's ministerial office. But it is good to be warned that this could be a case of reading more into the Latin text than what it had intended.[52] At any rate, "heavenly" is a curious description of ecclesiastical office. Probably under the influence of *rudimenta fidei*, several translations in other languages interpret *superni munus rudimenta* as "rudiments of Christian doctrine." These rudiments are what the church had received from the apostles.

The Collect for the Dedication of the Basilicas of Saints Peter and Paul (November 18) affirms pretty much the same thing: "as she [church] received from them [Saints Peter and Paul] / the beginnings of her knowledge of things divine, / so through them she may receive, / even to the end of the world, / an increase in heavenly grace."

The following is a literal translation of the Collect for the Solemnity of Saints Peter and Paul. It takes into account the foregoing discussion and the way the phrase *superni munus rudimenta* is rendered in other languages:

> Grant us, we pray, Lord our God,
> to be sustained by the intercession
> of the blessed apostles Peter and Paul,
> that through whom you gave your Church
> the rudiments of heavenly gift,
> through them you will extend the help
> of eternal salvation.

> The sense of the passage is "Through the apostles Peter and Paul God gave to the church in its early stages of growth the rudiments of faith or Christian doctrine."

Homiletic-Catechetical Note

It is said that Scripture and tradition embody everything that God has revealed to the church through Jesus Christ. After the last apostle had died, nothing more was added to the pages of Scripture or to the original body of tradition.

However, the Collect lets us know that what the apostles handed over to the church were rudiments of faith. Down the centuries the church, under the guidance of the Holy Spirit, not only preserved them but also made explicit what lay implicit in the deposit of Christian faith. Today the church continues to do both, conscious of its responsibility to the apostles, for it was through them that God had entrusted to the church the rudiments of faith.

The church comes from the apostles. It can claim two thousand years of life as a divine-human institution. Yet it knows that it must live in the present age treading the world's path of progress and poverty, technology and ignorance, faith and unbelief. The church continues to learn new things with humility as it pursues its mission to be in the world without being entrenched in its ways. It relies on the strength of the faith it received through the apostles.

The Constitution on the Sacred Liturgy (23) offers to the church a principle that balances its duty to preserve its apostolic institutions and its obligation to grow in its life of faith: sound tradition is to be retained, and yet the way is to remain open to legitimate progress.

Prayer after Communion
Saints Joachim and Anne, July 26

O God, who willed that your Only Begotten Son
should be born from among humanity
so that by a wonderful mystery
humanity might be born again from you,
we pray that, in your kindness,
you may sanctify by the spirit of adoption
those you have fed with the Bread you give your children.

> 1. born from among humanity
> 2. humanity might be born again

Interpretation of the Text

"Humanity" or humankind is a collective abstract noun. It should be pointed out that the Latin text uses a concrete noun, *homines*: men, women, and children. Although the first meaning of humanity is humankind, it frequently denotes the quality of being human or humane. It is not expedient to translate a concrete noun with an abstract noun.

It is, therefore, necessary to explain that "humanity" here refers to humans or human beings in the reality of flesh and blood, body and soul, mind and spirit. The incarnation of the Son of God involved not an abstract humanity but real humans of flesh and blood. He took on our humanity in and from the womb of a woman, herself born from humans.

The ancestral lineage of Jesus, according to the Gospel of Matthew, goes back to Abraham. It is in this broad sense that we are to interpret the oration's statement that God's only-begotten Son was born from humans, that is, he comes from a long line of human ancestors. But his only human parent was his mother. The following is a literal translation of this prayer:

> O God, who willed that your Only Begotten
> should be born from humans,
> so that by a wonderful mystery
> humans might be reborn from you,
> we pray that in your kindness
> you will sanctify by the spirit of adoption
> those you have fed with the bread of children.

The sense of this Prayer after Communion is "The Son of God was born from humans, so that by a wonderful mystery humans might be reborn from God."

Homiletic-Catechetical Note

The Collect is careful to say that of Saints Joachim and Anne the mother of God's incarnate Son was born. The logical conclusion that they were the grandparents of Jesus is not pursued. They were not directly and personally involved in the mystery of the incarnation. It was a divine affair between their daughter and the Holy Spirit.

On the other hand, the Prayer after Communion pursues another line of thought. It opens wide the mystery to the entire human race, not in an abstract way but concretely as human beings. His body and soul, his heart and spirit, his culture: all this came from us humans through his mother. When people gazed on him, heard him speak, and touched him, they saw and felt their own humanness, which the incarnate Word had taken on himself in order to heal, sanctify, and present to God for adoption.

The phrase "bread of children" recalls the words of Jesus to the Syrophoenician woman (Mark 7:27): "Let the children be fed first. For it is not right to take the food of the children and throw it to the dogs." The astounding effect of the mystery of the incarnation is that we were given "power to become children of God, . . . who were born not by natural generation nor by human choice nor by a man's decision but of God" (John 1:12-13). As children, we are fed with the "children's food."

Collect
The Transfiguration of the Lord, August 6

O God, who in the glorious Transfiguration
of your Only Begotten Son
confirmed the mysteries of faith by the witness of the Fathers
and wonderfully prefigured our full adoption to sonship,
grant, we pray, to your servants,
that, listening to the voice of your beloved Son,
we may merit to become co-heirs with him.

> 1. confirmed the mysteries of faith
> 2. by the witness of the Fathers

Interpretation of the Text

This Collect is the gospel of the transfiguration according to Luke (9:28-36) in prayer form.[53] The passage "confirmed the mysteries of faith" suggests Luke 9:31: Moses and Elijah "appeared in glory and spoke of his exodus that he was going to accomplish in Jerusalem." The subject of their conversation was Christ's "exodus" (in Greek, *éxodos*). With respect to him, "exodus" was his *pascha* or passage from this world to the Father, or, in a word, his paschal mystery. Hence, in this particular oration "mysteries of faith," which appropriately translates *fidei sacramenta*, means the paschal mystery of Christ's passion, death, and resurrection.[54]

The "witness of the Fathers" is *patrum testimonio* in the Latin oration. Who are these Fathers? According to the biblical narrative, they are Moses and Elijah. *Patres* may be suitably rendered in English as "ancestors," and, in the context of this oration, as "prophets."[55] The following is a literal translation of the oration:

110

O God, who in the glorious Transfiguration of your Only
  Begotten
confirmed the mystery of faith by the witness of the prophets
and prefigured the perfect adoption of children,
grant to us, your servants,
that listening to the voice of your beloved Son,
we may merit to be made his coheirs.

> The sense of the oration is "In the transfiguration
> of Christ, our belief in the paschal mystery was
> strengthened, and our adoption as children of God
> was foreshadowed."

Homiletic-Catechetical Note

The Collect of the Transfiguration is a prayer based on the Gospel of
Luke, which narrates what took place on the mountain. The chief person-
ages are Jesus and the two prophets Moses and Elijah representing the
ancestors. The three were conversing together about Christ's exodus, his
passage from this world to the Father. We know what that passage en-
tailed: betrayal, suffering, and ignominious death on a cross. That was
what Moses and Elijah were discussing with him on Mount Tabor at the
very moment when he was robed in the splendor and shone with the
radiance of his future glory.

Thus as Christ was enjoying a foretaste of the resurrection, the cross
cast its long and menacing shadow. So long as he was on earth, his life
would be an interplay of light and shadow. His life was never merely an
experience of light nor merely of shadow; it was an uneasy mingling of
both.

Later, on another mountain, on Mount Calvary, all marks of his divinity would fade away, his own Father would seem to have abandoned him,
and the two people who stood by him would no longer be Moses and
Elijah in their glory, but his grieving Mother and his Beloved Disciple.
We know that at that moment he was lifted up above the earth: it was his
moment of glory. On Tabor the cross dimmed his glory; on Calvary his
glory shone through the cross.

Christ's transfiguration foreshadowed our adoption as daughters and sons of God. Baptism vests us with the splendor of Christ, with the white unsullied garb of innocence and glory, so that God recognizes in us the countenance of the beloved Son. Baptism is the sacrament of our transfiguration. Every Second Sunday of Lent the liturgy presents to catechumens and faithful alike the icon of the transfigured Lord, reminding them of their baptism.

Collect
The Nativity of the Blessed Virgin Mary, September 8

Impart to your servants, we pray, O Lord,
the gift of heavenly grace,
that the feast of the Nativity of the Blessed Virgin
may bring deeper peace
to those for whom the birth of her Son
was the dawning of salvation.

> 1. the birth of her Son
> 2. the dawning of salvation

Interpretation of the Text

The Collect translates *Virginis partus* as "the birth of her Son." The title of Mary as Virgin is overlooked in the translation, though presumably it is understood. The literal translation is "childbirth of the Virgin." However, in homily and catechesis the doctrine "virgo ante partum, virgo in partu, et virgo post partum" is not to be neglected. It is our belief that Mary was virgin before, at, and after the childbirth of her Son. The Latin text teaches that she remained a virgin at childbirth.

The Collect rightly states that the childbirth of the Blessed Virgin Mary is "the dawning of salvation." Another possible translation is "The Blessed Virgin, by her childbirth, was the dawning of salvation."[56] This finds support in the Prayer after Communion: the church "rejoices in the Nativity of the Blessed Virgin Mary, / which was the hope and the daybreak of salvation." Below is a literal translation of the Collect:

Impart to your servants, we pray, O Lord,
the gift of heavenly grace,
that to those for whom the childbirth of the Virgin
was the beginning of salvation
the feast of her Nativity may yield an increase of peace.

> The sense of the passage is "We recognize in the childbirth of the Virgin Mary the beginning of salvation" or "Mary, by her virginal childbirth, brought about the dawning of salvation."

Homiletic-Catechetical Note

Jesus, Mary, and John the Baptist were born for a divine mission, for the fulfillment of a divine task. These are the only three persons whose birthday in the flesh is celebrated by the church. The other birthdays kept by the liturgical calendar are called *natale* or birthday to eternal life.

John the Baptist was born to be the precursor of the Lord. Once Jesus had been made known, he became like the moon whose light dims at the dawn of day. His satisfaction in life was to see his disciples leave him in order to follow Christ. The Lord Jesus himself was born in order to die. He longed to be baptized, that is, to undergo the torment of death. All his life he directed his gaze toward the hill outside the city of Jerusalem.

The Blessed Virgin was born to be the Mother of the Savior. She was a person who did not exist for herself; she existed only for her Son. Her fulfillment in life was to prepare her Son for his mission. When she accepted to be the Mother of Jesus, she embarked on a pilgrimage that led her to the foot of the cross. She did not understand everything in God's plan and the death of her Son must have remained a mystery to her, but she did not waver in her belief that whatever the outcome, her God was a God who cared.

When we celebrate the Nativity of the Blessed Virgin Mary, we direct our thoughts to the other Nativity that her birth heralded and to the other Person that endowed her life with meaning.

Collect
All Saints, November 1

Almighty ever-living God,
by whose gift we venerate in one celebration
the merits of all the Saints,
bestow on us, we pray,
through the prayers of so many intercessors,
an abundance of the reconciliation with you
for which we earnestly long.

> an abundance of the reconciliation with you

Interpretation of the Text

What does "abundance of the reconciliation" mean? The Latin is *tuae propitiationis abundantiam* or "richness of your mercy." *Propitius* and *propitiatio* are some of the oldest Latin terms frequently employed to denote the human sentiment of trust in the goodness of God.[57] The adjective *propitius* is used so that God will be favorably disposed to grant the petition. *Propitiatio* often refers to God's kindhearted disposition. Thus, "reconciliation" does not adequately render the sense of the Latin word. The following is a literal translation of the oration:

Almighty ever-living God,
who willed that we honor in one feast
the merits of all your Saints,
we pray that, by the intercession of so many,
you will grant us the abundance of your mercy
for which we long.

> The sense of the phrase is "With a great multitude
> of saints praying for us, we can long for God's out-
> pouring of mercy."

Homiletic-Catechetical Note

According to the Constitution on the Sacred Liturgy, "The church has also included memorial days of the martyrs and other saints in the annual cycle. . . . By celebrating the days on which they died, the church proclaims the paschal mystery in the saints who have suffered and have been glorified with Christ. It proposes them to the faithful as models who draw all people to the Father through Christ, and through their merits it begs for God's favor" (104).

To such an exalted doctrine the Collect for All Saints affixes a consideration quite human in its motivation. We trust that God will listen to our prayer, because a countless number of saints surround God in the heavenly court, all interceding on our behalf. There is strength in numbers.

The Collect echoes the Litany of the Saints wherein we invoke with urgency so many saints on whose special prayers we can rely. It is not unusual that people who find themselves in trying situations call upon many saints for assistance and deliverance.

Such human consideration surfaces again in the Prayer over the Offerings. The saints in heaven are "already assured of immortality." Their earthly struggles are ended; now they can devote themselves fully to the affairs of their sisters and brothers here on earth. The oration strengthens our belief that those in the other life continue to commune with us, take interest in our world, and plead for us before the throne of God.

Throughout the pages of the Roman Missal we meet similar human motivation and logic. Liturgical prayers every so often address the heart more than the intellect. They cross the perimeter that normally distinguishes official worship from popular piety. They allow the heart to speak; they bestow on liturgical worship a human quality.

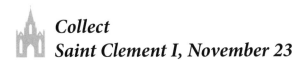

Collect
Saint Clement I, November 23

Almighty ever-living God,
who are wonderful in the virtue of all your Saints,
grant us joy in the yearly commemoration of Saint Clement,
who, as a Martyr and High Priest of your Son,
bore out by his witness what he celebrated in mystery
and confirmed by example what he preached with his lips.

> 1. High Priest of your Son
> 2. what he celebrated in mystery / and confirmed
>   by example

Interpretation of the Text

We are familiar with the designation of the pope as Supreme Pontiff or High Priest. What does "High Priest" mean in this Collect? The Latin text is *sacerdos* without the adjective *magnus*. "Drawn from the sacral language of Rome, *sacerdos* had, in Early Christian Latin, no hierarchical meaning as did *episcopus*, *presbyter*, and *diaconus*; but it simply designated 'one who performed the priestly functions', 'a mediator between God and man'. In the orations it is used to designate a bishop."[58] In light of a later development regarding the use of *sacerdos*, the English translation may not be literal, but it is contextual.[59]

The passage "what he celebrated in mystery" is a clear allusion to the liturgical rite that the saint offered in his capacity as priest. Here the Latin oration brilliantly employs the antithetical device in four segments: "quod mysterio gessit, testimonio comprobavit, et, quod praedicavit ore, confirmavit exemplo."

> The sense of the Collect is "As bishop and martyr
> for your Son, Saint Clement celebrated the sacred
> liturgy to which he bore witness by preaching and
> example of life."

Homiletic-Catechetical Note

The offering of the Eucharist or its celebration "in mystery" is done
through the ministry of the priest. The Collect calls our attention to the
relationship between the mystery and the witnessing thereof (*mysterium/
martyrium*) in the person of Pope Saint Clement, bishop and martyr. By
God's grace he confirmed the truth and efficacy of what he celebrated by
word and deed. His shedding of blood corroborated his testimony.

The doctrine of the church requires priestly ordination for presiding
at the celebration of the eucharistic sacrifice. For participating in it, the
same requires the sacrament of baptism whereby the faithful are incor-
porated into the priestly people (1 Pet 2:9). The Constitution on the Sacred
Liturgy is apropos: "It is very much the wish of the church that all the
faithful should be led to take that full, conscious, and active part in liturgical celebrations which is demanded by the very nature of the liturgy,
and to which the Christian people, 'a chosen race, a royal priesthood, a
holy nation, a redeemed people' (1 Pet 2:9, 4-5) have a right and to which
they are bound by reason of their Baptism" (14).

In the celebration of the Eucharist the ordained priest and baptized
faithful come together to exercise their respective priestly duties. They
offer "in mystery" the one sacrifice of Christ: the priest *in persona Christi*;
the faithful with and through the priest. Baptismal or common priesthood
finds its highest expression in participation in the eucharistic liturgy.
Together with the priest, they too are called to celebrate the mystery in
liturgical rite and manner of life.

Collect
The Immaculate Conception
of the Blessed Virgin Mary, December 8

O God, who by the Immaculate Conception of the
    Blessed Virgin
prepared a worthy dwelling for your Son,
grant, we pray,
that, as you preserved her from every stain
by virtue of the Death of your Son, which you foresaw,
so, through her intercession,
we, too, may be cleansed and admitted to your presence.

> we, too, may be cleansed

Interpretation of the Text

The passage "we, too, may be cleansed" does not mean that the Blessed Virgin Mary was cleansed of sin. She was not cleansed: she was preserved from sin. This is the doctrine of the immaculate conception. In the English text the adverb "too," meaning "also," is misplaced and may cause doctrinal confusion.

The Latin text is admittedly a tricky one to translate: *nos quoque mundos*. The adjective *mundos* (clean) defines *nos* (we). *Mundos* is not a past participle (*mundatos*). The Latin phrase does not say *nos quoque mundatos*. The problem at hand is caused by the translation of *mundos* as a verbal clause (may be cleansed) rather than simply an adjective (clean). In fairness to the English version, a literal translation of the Latin would sound awkward: "We too, clean, may be admitted to your presence." Nonetheless, the present English text could raise doctrinal debate. It needs to be correctly interpreted or, better, reformed.

Here is a literal translation of the Collect:

> O God, who through the Immaculate Conception of the Virgin
> prepared a worthy dwelling for your Son,
> we beg you, who preserved her from every stain
> because of the foreseen death of your Son,
> to grant by her intercession
> that we who have been made clean may also appear before you.

> The sense of the phrase is "By the intercession of Mary, may we be cleansed of our sins and thus may also reach our heavenly home."

Homiletic-Catechetical Note

This Collect was composed in 1477. The 1854 dogmatic decree *Ineffabilis Deus* by Pope Pius IX echoes it: "By a singular grace and privilege of Almighty God, and in view of the merits of Jesus Christ, Savior of the human race, Mary was preserved free from all stain of original sin."

The Collect teaches that the immaculate conception of Mary was God's means of preparing her to be the Mother of the incarnate Word. In fact, this was the reason why Catholic theology reached the conclusion that Mary, the preordained Mother of God, had to be conceived without sin. The key phrase is *morte praevisa* (because of Christ's foreseen death), which the pope reworded so as to encompass all the merits of Christ the Savior: *praevisis meritis*. Mary, like all of us, was redeemed by her Son, but unlike us she, by a special privilege as the future Mother of God, enjoyed the benefit of her Son's saving work even before he had accomplished it.

"Preserved . . . from every stain" of sin, Mary did not have the root cause of sin or the natural weakness that leads to sin. This does not mean that she did not enjoy the basic freedom of every human being; what it means is that she used that freedom spontaneously to grow in holiness of life. Mary was already redeemed at her conception, but she was always in need of God's sustaining grace in order to remain without sin. Like all of us, Mary struggled to stay in God's grace, to understand God's will, and to grow in love of God and neighbor. In his encyclical letter *Redemptoris Mater* Pope John Paul II named her "Pilgrim of Faith." Her immaculate conception did not set her apart from us, but gave us a model to imitate in our journey as pilgrims of faith.

Mary was preserved from original sin because of her unique role as Mother of God. We, on the other hand, were subjected to the wiles of sin from the moment we were conceived. That is why we beg for the grace of God to cleanse us of sin. We pray, putting our trust in a mother who intercedes for her other children. After all, her being mother of us all is a task that completes her primary role of being Mother of God. Jesus himself affirmed it in his parting words to her: "Behold, your son."

Notes

1. There are several studies on the new English Order of Mass. The 694-page volume *A Commentary on the Order of Mass of* The Roman Missal (Collegeville, MN: Liturgical Press, 2011), edited by E. Foley, is a scholarly and pastoral treatise.

2. A similar approach to the orations in the Roman Missal is done in Spanish by C. Urtasun: *Las oraciones del misal* (Barcelona: Centro de Pastoral Litúrgica, 1995). The author extensively analyzes the presidential prayers, compares the Spanish translation with other European languages, and offers meditations on each oration.

3. Three classic works on liturgical Latin are C. Mohrmann, *Études sur le latin des chrétiens* (Rome: Edizioni di storia e letteratura, 1958); *Liturgical Latin, Its Origins and Character* (Washington, DC: Catholic University of America Press, 1957); M. P. Ellebracht, *Remarks on the Vocabulary of the Ancient Orations in the Missale Romanum* (Nijmegen: Dekker, 1963); and A. Blaise, *Le vocabulaire latin des principaux thèmes liturgiques* (Turnhout: Brepols, 1966).

4. R. Foster and D. McCarthy, "*Collectarum latinitas*," in *Appreciating the Collect: An Irenic Methodology*, ed. J. Leachman and D. McCarthy, 27–56 (Farnborough, England: St. Michael's Abbey Press, 2008); R. De Zan, "How to Interpret a Collect," in *Appreciating the Collect*, 57–82; De Zan, "Criticism and Interpretation of Liturgical Texts," in *Handbook for Liturgical Studies*, vol. I, ed. A. Chupungco, 331–65 (Collegeville, MN: Liturgical Press, 1997). Although the two previously cited works deal mostly with the collect, the principles and criteria they advance can apply to Latin orations in general. See also P. Regan, "The Collect in Context," in *Appreciating the Collect*, 83–99.

5. De Zan, "Criticism and Interpretation of Liturgical Texts," 75.

6. C. Vagaggini, *Theological Dimensions of the Liturgy* (Collegeville, MN: Liturgical Press, 1976): "Christ as head of his members assumes responsibility before God, so to speak, for the performance of the prayer and the rite which he by special mandate has given power to the hierarchy to institute and to perform in his name as head of the Church."

7. Ellebracht, *Remarks on the Vocabulary*, 201: "In the orations it [*quaesumus*] is always found in the one form, namely the first person plural of the present indicative. *Da, Fac, Praesta, Concede, Intende, Accipe*, and the rest, are invariably followed by this word which already in pre-classical Latin was enclitic. Thus, *quaesumus* serves a double function: it tones down the imperative, which man has no right to direct to God, and it enhances the rhythm."

8. Much has been written on this topic. Ellebracht, *Remarks on the Vocabulary*, 67–71, gives a comprehensive summary. See also M. Collins and E. Foley, "Mystagogy: Discerning the Mystery of Faith," *A Commentary on the Order of Mass*, 73–102.

9. Ellebracht, *Remarks on the Vocabulary*, 71.

10. "Instances where *devotio* is used in one or other genitive construction with words for the sacred action display the cultic sense of the term . . . Secret prayers often deal with the sacramental character of the sacred rites" (Ellebracht, *Remarks on the Vocabulary*, 98).

11. According to Blaise (*Le vocabulaire latin*, 63, 120), the meaning of *peragere* in this oration is "to celebrate in a rite." *Instituta sacri mysterii* means the institution of the Eucharist.

12. Ellebracht, *Remarks on the Vocabulary*, 58; see also Blaise, *Le vocabulaire latin*, 369.

13. "The adjective *solemnis* means 'annual,' and it was applied in pagan Latin especially to religious feasts and the games . . . *Sollemnia* [*dominica sollemnia*] stands for the ritual action . . . In two instances it is applied to the feast of Christmas" (Ellebracht, *Remarks on the Vocabulary*, 112–13).

14. Etymologically, liturgy means service. It is helpful to note that the Latin version of the third-century *Apostolic Tradition* (no. 3), attributed to Hippolytus of Rome, translates *leitourgounta* with *servientem*. Indeed, the notion of service is essential to the definition of liturgy.

15. Quotations from the documents of the Second Vatican Council are taken from Austin Flannery, *Vatican Council II: The Basic Sixteen Documents* (Northport, NY: Costello, 1996).

16. See D. McCarthy and J. Leachman's analysis of this collect in *Listen to the Word: Commentaries on Selected Opening Prayers of Sundays and Feasts with Sample Homilies* (London: Tablet, 2009), 9–10; Blaise translates it as *vouloir bien* (*Le vocabulaire latin*, 174).

17. See A. Echiegu's exegesis of this collect: *Translating the Collects of the "Sollemnitates Domini" of the "Missale Romanum" of Paul VI in the Language of the African* (Münster: Regensberg, 1984), 123–227.

18. Ellebracht, *Remarks on the Vocabulary*, 198–99.

19. Ibid., 176: "Only once does this noun [*praesidium*] appear in the orations in an evident military figure: *Concede nobis . . . praesidia militiae Christianae sanctis inchoare jejuniis.* In this phrase it is used by metonymy: the garrison for the warfare itself."

20. See, however, R. Tuzik's endorsement of the translation of *praesidia* as campaign in his book *Praying the Roman Missal* (Chicago: Liturgy Training Publications, 2011), 19–20.

21. Timothy Fry, ed., *RB 1980: The Rule of St. Benedict in Latin and English with Notes* (Collegeville, MN: Liturgical Press, 1981).

22. Blaise, *Le vocabulaire latin*, 41.

23. See McCarthy, *Listen to the Word*, 15–18.

24. An important research tool for the origins of the orations in the 1975 Roman Missal is the work of C. Johnson and A. Ward, *Missale Romanum anno 1975 promulgatum: orationes et benedictiones* (Rome: CLV, 1994); for the sources of the Prefaces, see the comprehensive work of the same authors: *The Prefaces of the Roman Missal* (Rome: Tipografia Poliglotta Vaticana, 1989).

25. See M. Metzger, "The History of the Roman Eucharistic Liturgy in Rome," in *Handbook for Liturgical Studies*, vol. III, ed. A. Chupungco, 109–14 (Collegeville, MN: Liturgical Press, 1999).

26. McCarthy, *Listen to the Word*, 15.

27. Metzger, "History of the Roman Eucharistic Liturgy," 111–12.

28. "In the secret for Ash Wednesday we are represented as celebrating by the Eucharist the beginning of the Paschal mystery, which is called *venerabile sacramentum*" (Ellebracht, *Remarks on the Vocabulary*, 72).

29. Ibid., 146–47.

30. *Traditio* in this oration alludes to the words of Jesus at the Last Supper: "Do this in my memory" (see Blaise, *Le vocabulaire latin*, 382–84).

31. Ibid., 110.

32. *General Instruction of the Roman Missal*, Third Typical Edition (2002), 303.

33. Ibid., 296.

34. Blaise, *Le vocabulaire latin*, 129: "*ce que nous avons commencé à célébrer du mystère pascal.*"

35. Ellebracht, *Remarks on the Vocabulary*, 186.

36. Collect (Monday within the Octave of Easter, Monday after the Third Sunday of Easter, Saturday after the Fourth Week of Easter), Prayer over the Offerings (Fourth Sunday of Lent, Wednesday of the Fifth Week of Lent), and Prayer after Communion (Wednesday of the Fourth Week of Lent).

37. Blaise, *Le vocabulaire latin*, 399–400; Ellebracht, *Remarks on the Vocabulary*, 186–87.

38. Ignatius of Antioch, *Letter to the Ephesians*, 20, 2.

39. *On the Sacraments* IV, 6, 28. In this connection the *Catechism of the Catholic Church* (1395) reminds us that "the Eucharist is not ordered to the forgiveness of mortal sins—that is proper to the sacrament of Reconciliation."

40. McCarthy analyzes at length the literary form of this collect in his book *Listen to the Word*, 53–54.

41. G. Moore, "The Vocabulary of the Collects," in *Appreciating the Collect*, 184–86. See C. Mohrmann, "*Rationabilis–Logikos*," *Études*, 179; Blaise, *Le vocabulaire latin*, 476; and Ellebracht, *Remarks on the Vocabulary*, 18. Ellebracht notes that *rationabilis* in archaic Christian usage meant spiritual, but "it gradually underwent semantic change so that it came to mean 'reasonable, conformed to the essence of a thing.'" Both Ellebracht and Blaise agree that *rationabilis* in this oration means "spiritual."

42. Blaise, *Le vocabulaire latin*, 265–66.

43. McCarthy, *Listen to the Word*, 61–62. According to him, "This prayer for the eleventh Sunday in Ordinary Time shows how the Christian assembly acknowledges its dependence on God for every good deed."

44. The "reference to the praying assembly is indirect. The motive clause refers to all humanity when it says *mortalis infirmitas*, 'human weakness.' Thus, the prayer states the human condition without directly attributing weakness to the assembly" (ibid., 62).

45. Blaise, *Le vocabulaire latin*, 401. He translates this passage thus: "*puisque, faible mortels, nous ne pouvons rien sans vous.*"

46. McCarthy, *Listen to the Word*, 77.

47. Blaise discusses extensively the various titles of the Holy Trinity used in the orations: *Le vocabulaire latin*, 353–65. See McCarthy's analysis of this collect: *Listen to the Word*, 109–10.

48. Ellebracht, *Remarks on the Vocabulary*, 126; Blaise, *Le vocabulaire latin*, 491–94.

49. Blaise, *Le vocabulaire latin*, 393. Commenting on this oration, he writes, "*Ces offrandes sont un symbole mystique d'unité et de paix.*"

50. Blaise offers other words that are applicable in English to translate *magnificare*: ibid., 138.

51. Ellebracht, *Remarks on the Vocabulary*, 163–68.

52. The Spanish Missal translates it: *primicias de tu obra de salvación;* the Italian: *primizie della fede cristiana;* Portuguese: *os primeiros ensinamentos da fé;* and the French: *les premiers bienfaits de ta grâce.* See Urtasun, *Las oraciones del misal*, 712–13.

53. "The scriptural nucleus of the feast comes from Psalm 2:7" (McCarthy, *Listen to the Word*, 111).

54. See Ellebracht's explanation of the different meanings of *sacramenta* in liturgical usage. "In general we may say that in the Orations, as frequently in other Christian Latin works, the word *sacramentum* is almost synonymous with *mysterium*" (*Remarks on the Vocabulary*, 72).

55. See passim, Blaise, *Le vocabulaire latin*, 308.

56. This is the translation proposed by Blaise: "*La bienheureuse Vierge, par son enfantment, a été l'aurore du salut*" (ibid., 348).

57. Ellebracht, *Remarks on the Vocabulary*, 142–43.

58. Ibid., 148.

59. Blaise explains that in the Vulgate, *sacerdos* refers to Hebrew priests and that in the third Council of Carthage, *princeps sacerdotum* or *summus sacerdos* was used to designate a bishop. The title *summus sacerdos* is applied to the pope in the Prayer over the Offerings for a dead pope (formula B), 518–20.